A WORLD OF ANIMALS
THE SAN DIEGO ZOO AND THE WILD ANIMAL PARK

A WORLD O

THE SAN DIEGO ZOO AND

TEXT BY BILL BRUNS
FOREWORD BY JANE GOODALL
PHOTOGRAPHS BY RON GARRISON

HARRY N. ABRAMS, INC., PUBLISHERS, NEW YORK

F ANIMALS
THE WILD ANIMAL PARK

To my grandmothers, Allora Lawrence and Oral Ollestad

Project Manager: Margaret L. Kaplan
Editor: Sheila Franklin
Designer: Bob McKee

Library of Congress Cataloging in Publication Data

Bruns, Bill.
A world of animals.

Summary: Text and photographs introduce the San Diego Zoo and the Wild Animal Park, one of the world's ten best zoos, and its animals and the people who care for them.
1. San Diego Zoo.   [1. San Diego Zoo.
2. Zoological gardens]   I. Garrison, Ron, ill.
II. Title.
QL76.5.U62S2617 1983   590'.74'479498   83-7289
ISBN 0-8109-1601-0

Illustrations © 1983 by the Zoological Society of San Diego

Printed and bound in Japan

Title "zoonooz" registered U.S. Patent Office

CONTENTS

FOREWORD

The huge tree towered above me as I gazed at it in amazement. "But surely *no one* could actually transplant a tree this size," I said. "Why, its roots must go down for miles."

I was standing in one of the picnic areas of the San Diego Zoo. The tree was a splendid specimen of Senegal date palm (*Phoenix reclinata*) which had been bequeathed to the Zoo's outstanding botanical collection. And, I was assured by Sheldon Campbell, the president of the board of trustees, and Director Charlie Schroeder, that they had indeed dug up and relocated that tree—even though it had meant turning off the electricity of part of the city for a short time while they maneuvered the huge branches underneath an overhead power line.

That incident made a deep impression on me. This was no ordinary zoo, that could successfully tackle a problem of such magnitude. It was a zoo which, up to that time, had been highly successful: a zoo which obviously had a great future.

That was in 1966. I had been invited to attend the celebration of the Zoo's fiftieth birthday—to give a lecture and to cut the cake. I shall never forget that occasion. The birthday cake, covered with white frosting, stretched out along a row of trestle tables for no less than 100 yards! A cake as long as a football field! On both sides were children, their parents, and other

Zoo members: hundreds of smiling faces. By an extraordinary coincidence that day just happened to be *my* birthday, too (never mind which one!). I had not told anyone, but somehow they knew, and there, up at one end, was a separate cake for me, decorated with little chimps. Afterward, we took big chunks of cake to the chimps, gorillas, and orangs.

That first visit is still vivid in my memory. I became acquainted, for the first time, with a pygmy chimp named Kakowet. He was six years old then, and weighed 60 pounds. He was amazingly gentle compared with "common" chimps of his age that I'd met in other zoos. And, thanks to his industrious efforts at propagation, the San Diego Zoo now has the largest of the four pygmy chimp breeding colonies in captivity. Kakowet himself, sadly, has passed on to the Eternal Forest—but his memory lives on in his fine, healthy offspring.

During my visit, I was, of course, taken on a tour of the Zoo, and I was very impressed. The animals were healthy and supremely well cared for. I was shown the fruit and vegetable storerooms, which sported a mouth-watering array—things as fresh as and far more exotic than anything one would find except in the most exclusive of greengrocers. I peered through clouds of swirling ice-cold vapors at row upon row of hanging carcasses. The kitchens, where the food was prepared, were scrupulously clean and hygienic. Some animals have very specialized diets and the preparation of their food is not easy, but the staff is so expert that any of them could get a job in invalid cookery whenever they wanted! And, I would happily have laid myself out for an operation in the gleaming, sterile operating theater—a room I know something about, for my uncle was a consultant surgeon and on many occasions I'd been allowed into his theater to watch him operate. Everywhere, I met people who cared about animals, from the director to the keepers to the staff who served in the Zoo restaurant.

All that was a long, long time ago—nearly twenty years have passed and much has happened. The Zoo has moved from strength to strength, and every time I make a return visit (which I do as often as possible) there are new animals, new and better exhibits, and new and exciting management, research, and conservation projects.

During my last visit, for example, Chuck Bieler, the current director, and I walked around inside the spacious, almost completed enclosure for the orangutan group. Sheldon Campbell showed me the redecorated bird cages, where, by the addition of soil and vegetation, old-fashioned concrete-floored exhibits had been transformed into miniature wild habitats where one could stand for hours, watching the inhabitants flitting about their avian business. And these exhibits had been transformed at practically no cost by the keepers themselves by means of imagination and hard work.

I met some of the scientists of the Research Department, each one in the forefront of his field—behavior, genetics, endocrinology, pathology—each one bubbling over with enthusiasm for his particular research, and all of them dedicated to the development of increasingly sophisticated methods for trying to save endangered species from extinction. I was told about the large "Frozen Zoo," where semen, ova, and other cells are preserved. This material is mainly used in the artificial-insemination program, which enables captive breeding to proceed without the traumatic and costly shipment of animals between zoos. In addition, it serves as a "library" for geneticists.

The most dramatic development since my 1966 visit has been, of course, the San Diego Wild Animal Park in the San Pasqual Valley. The first time I went there it was not yet open to the public and was only half completed. As I drove around, looking at the herds of hoofed animals grazing peacefully, the golden hills—where the grass was bleached after the hot sun of summer—were reminiscent of parts of my beloved Tanzania. Since it was first opened, the Wild Animal Park has been an outstanding success, attracting literally a million or more visitors every year. What impresses me most—after the tranquillity of the scenery and the meticulous planning—is the fact that one is conveyed around the Park by monorail. This is free of the toxic and unpleasant gasoline fumes which must make life obnoxious in most of the "safari parks." And this is the hallmark of the San Diego Zoo—treat the public as welcome guests; look after them, entertain them, and educate them—but never at the expense of the animals. When scientists decided that the endangered African cheetah, which had proved almost impossible to breed in captivity, might do so in *undisturbed* conditions, the Zoo director unhesitatingly agreed to screen the potential breeding group from the public, despite the fact that it would be a good attraction. Thus, the cheetahs got the privacy they needed, and they bred successfully.

One of the bad aspects of zoos is that so often the more intelligent species become most terribly bored. All their wants are tended to and they have nothing to do except gaze at a succession of human faces. That is why I approve so wholeheartedly of the "shows" which visitors can enjoy in the amphitheater of the Wild Animal Park. Here, elephants, parrots, and even falcons perform daily. In particular the keepers who trained the parrots and cockatoos to perform their stunning act—one cockatoo named Pancho sings note-perfect opera—deserve the highest praise. My own memory of the amphitheater is rather different. I was asked to give an inaugural lecture there, one spring evening. As luck would have it, it was a cold, misty day, with rain threatening. There was a good audience, staunchly enduring an hour and a half on hard wooden benches, and they huddled into their coats and pressed close together for warmth. I stood in the open, wishing desperately I had heavier clothes as I talked about my tropical forest chimps. But Chuck Bieler, noticing how I shivered, gallantly flung his jacket around my shoulders. What fun it was!

Of course, I would rather see animals in the wild—that's why I live and work in Africa. But most people are not so lucky—they can have firsthand experience of wild animals only by going to a zoo. And I believe, most definitely, that we *need* zoos—good zoos like the one at San Diego. Especially for children. A child lives in a world that is half fantasy: for one thing, he has a vivid imagination; for another, we feed him stories of dragons and all manner of magical and mythical beasts. How can he be expected to know, when he hears about a giraffe or a rhino, or sees pictures, that *these* are "for real"? He cannot—not until he sees them with his own eyes, hears them, smells them, and so knows them from his own senses.

The San Diego Zoo has excellent educational programs for young people. The most important of these, I believe, is the Children's Zoo, where a child can actually touch the animals, relate to them as personalities, visit them again and again, and watch them grow up. Children have a great capacity for simply standing and watching an animal. How often, as one walks around a zoo, does one hear parents or teachers urging their charges: "Come on, it's time to see some *other* animals." This always makes me angry—the child knows so much better how to derive maximum enjoyment and advantage from a visit to the zoo. He should be allowed to watch and absorb as much as he wants, for it is the children of today who will, ultimately, determine the fate of so many of the animals that we, as adults, are fighting to save from extinction. And only when people know and understand animals, realize their value as fellow travelers on planet Earth, will they be *really* motivated to help in conservation efforts.

Conservation of animal species should be a major concern of all civilized people, whether it be for ethical, aesthetic, or sentimental reasons—or even for purely economic ones. Animal and plant species are disappearing at a truly alarming rate, and the chain of life in nature is so complex that we cannot really predict the impact on our environment if such depredations are allowed to continue unabated. Many zoos are now active in the conservation field and, of course, one of their major goals is the breeding of endangered species. So many natural habitats, especially forest ones, are vanishing at a terrifying speed that, while fighting desperately to preserve at least some areas where animals can live natural lives in the wild, it is also necessary to gather up some of the refugees, offer them the best conditions possible, and try to breed them. The San Diego Zoo, as one would predict, is playing a leading role in this field. Seventeen of the twenty-five endangered species in its collection have bred, some regularly. The pygmy chimps and the cheetahs are but two examples.

It is the hope of all nature lovers that, one day, sufficient areas of wilderness throughout the world will be set aside for the creatures with whom we share the earth. Then, perhaps, animals which have been bred in captivity may once again know the exhilaration—and dangers—of freedom. In the meantime, there are dedicated people to look after those which have found refuge in zoos around the world. If I were one of those refugees I would consider myself lucky to be offered hospitality by the San Diego Zoo.

Jane Goodall

HISTORY OF
THE SAN DIEGO
ZOO

When the fledgling San Diego Zoo acquired its first elephants in 1923, a pair of females from India named Empress and Queenie, Director Harry Wegeforth had to hire a railroad baggage car to bring them down from San Francisco. In *It Began with a Roar,* by Neil Morgan, Wegeforth described what happened when the elephants arrived at the station:

We placed a heavy sheet of iron between the car and the unloading platform, and the elephants walked over that meekly. Then they decided they had been pushed around enough on their long trip from India . . . and so they staged a stand-up strike—just stood there, immovable. Chains had been put on their legs so they couldn't move too far in the wrong direction—an unnecessary precaution since they weren't inclined to move in any direction. We pushed and pulled with an elephant hook, but staunch as Gibraltar they remained.

At last it occurred to me that they probably were accustomed to being ridden. Ready to resort to anything, I climbed up on Empress and found that by kicking her on the side of the head, I could get her to move. I could get her to go in the direction I wanted by pushing with the bullhook behind her ear or pulling back from the front of the ear.

Harry Edwards, one of the men from the Zoo, mounted Queenie and found the same code worked. Then we had the chains taken off

their legs. Feeling like Indian rajahs and also pretty silly, we rode through the city. More than one driver slammed on his brakes when he saw those huge animals looming out of the dark on the familiar streets of San Diego!

That Harry Wegeforth (pronounced Way-ga-forth) should find himself astride an Asian elephant, delivering it to his own zoo, would have come as little surprise to those who knew him as a youngster back in Baltimore. Born in 1882, he had a keen interest in animals that went much deeper than the usual childhood fascination with unusual creatures. He maintained extensive snake and turtle collections at home, researched the habits and characteristics of all types of animals, and even learned to play a fife solely to keep his pet pigeon happy. Moreover, he developed a skill in selling and trading animals that would later stand him in good stead as he set about building the San Diego Zoo's collection. One Baltimore neighbor from those early years remembers young Harry—his necktie flamboyantly knotted around his leg—managing to sell her three garter snakes at a very healthy price, even though she had very little love of snakes.

At the age of twelve, fascinated by the itinerant circus shows that visited Baltimore, Harry spent the winter learning to walk the high wire with a troop of circus performers encamped near

Founder Dr. Harry Wegeforth
astride one of the Asian elephants which arrived at the Zoo
in 1923

his home. Within a year, he had become proficient enough to join their act, actually accompanying them when they left town; but this particular dream was soon ended when an older brother followed him and brought him back home.

Wegeforth returned to school, but only briefly. When he was sixteen, he headed West on his own—partly to recover from tuberculosis but mostly to satisfy his longing for foot-loose adventure. He spent almost four years as a cowpuncher on the high plains of Colorado, completing his high-school education by mail, and then returned to Baltimore to begin studying for a medical degree. Although he eventually landed an important post in surgery, he was unable to subdue his yearnings for the West. So, in 1908, he left town, heading first for Seattle and eventually for San Diego, seduced by the warm, dry weather of that beautiful port city.

Wegeforth adopted San Diego with great fervor. He had no trouble in establishing a thriving medical practice (as an orthopedic surgeon, he was soon considered *the* doctor to see) or in persuading his sister, Emma, and two of his brothers, Paul and Arthur, to join him. In 1912, he was appointed president of the city's board of health, and was later named to the board of directors for San Diego's gala Panama-California International Exposition of 1915–16, a world's fair held at Balboa Park (a 1,400-acre tract of land in the center of the city) that was designed to boost the city's reputation.

One exposition attraction was a rather motley collection of borrowed animals exhibited in a string of makeshift cages. The plan was to return the animals and tear down the cages as soon as the exposition ended—until the day, that is, when Wegeforth and his brother Paul, driving near the menagerie, happened to hear the lions roaring. Founding a zoological society had been in the back of Harry's mind for quite some time, but now the idea crystallized. As he later recalled, "I turned to my brother and, half-jokingly, half-wishfully said, 'Wouldn't it be splendid if San Diego had a zoo! You know . . . I think I'll start one.' "

Wegeforth proceeded to drive to *The San Diego Union,* where he talked to the city editor, and the next morning (September 27, 1916), an article appeared announcing Wegeforth's intention to develop a "zoological garden," starting with the animals from the exposition's collection. A week later, five people—four physicians and one naturalist—met to spell out a series of objectives that were, indeed, farsighted. The directors drew up bylaws that promised, among other things, to collect animals and plants in a zoological garden "for the instruction, recreation, and pleasure of the public and for scientific study; and to promote all branches of natural history, actively engage in biological research and participate in wild animal conservation."

These dreams would all become realities in the future, but in October, 1916, the directors were intent on simply finding a permanent location for their zoo (a task which was to involve them in a six-year-long struggle with the city) and obtaining some animals.

Dr. Harry Wegeforth was a man who tackled projects with vigorous enthusiasm and boundless optimism, and he would need both of these qualities—and many more—as he fought to keep his young zoo alive through the many crises that beset it during the next fifteen years. He would later admit that he did not fully realize what he was getting into, and that he did not have a fully formed idea of what the San Diego Zoo would become. In the beginning, it was simply his love of animals and his community spirit that prompted him to spend all of his spare time on behalf of the Zoo, yet he was probably the only man in town who possessed all the personal characteristics necessary to make a zoo grow and prosper in San Diego. He persevered in building the Zoo when others were prepared to lose heart because it simply did not occur to him that such a project might fail. If there seemed to be little public interest in a zoo, he had more than enough passion about animals and more than enough talent as a showman to generate that interest. If most people thought that San Diego was an inappropriate locale for a major zoo, removed as it was from major population centers, he knew that it had the best climate in the United States for raising exotic animals out of doors—and he had faith that the city would grow. Finally, though there appeared to be very little money available locally to fund such an ambitious undertaking, he would soon reveal an ability not only to find money but to separate people from it, thus becoming somewhat of a local legend.

As a first step in all that was to come, Wegeforth paid $500 in cash for most of the exposition animals, and the city council then handed over the string of rickety cages in which the animals had been living. (These living conditions did not really improve over the next five-and-a-half years, despite Wege-

These wolf cages along Park Boulevard were left over from the Panama-California International Exposition in 1916 and comprised part of the early Zoo, before it moved to its present location in Balboa Park in 1922.

forth's efforts to gain financial support for a plan to move the animals into barless enclosures and grottoes similar to those pioneered by the Hagenbeck Zoo in Hamburg, Germany.) The city also assigned to the Society small groups of animals kept in other parts of Balboa Park, including some bison, a pair of bears, and small herds of elk and Panama deer.

Once this basic animal collection was secured, money became a formidable problem. "I cannot remember a time in the early days of the Zoo when we were not in financial straits," Wegeforth later wrote. That this was the case is more than illustrated by the balance sheets for February, 1917. Expenses for the month totaled a modest $95.67; of this sum $45 was spent on a keeper's salary, $5.25 on horsemeat for two animals, $9.42 on 156 loaves of bread, $5 on 4 bags of carrots, $29.90 on 2,500 pounds of hay, 60¢ on drinking pans, and 50¢ on medicine. Unfortunately, income for the month was only $15—and this a contribution from the city's park commission.

Budget problems grew even more dire as the Zoo began to fall heir to substantial numbers of wild animals. Ordinary citizens wandered into Wegeforth's medical offices with pelicans, sea lions, and other local wildlife that the owners could no longer handle, such as rattlesnakes, opossums, and bobcats. Meanwhile, sailors from the U.S. naval base in San Diego brought in parrots, monkeys, boa constrictors, and coatimundis (raccoon-like omnivores) which had become too large or obstreperous to remain on shipboard as pets.

One memorable gift during this period was a female Kodiak bear, given by the crew of the U.S. collier *Nanshan*. Misnamed "Caesar," this handsome bear had been popular with everyone on the boat until, one day, she became a little too playful and knocked the captain into a nearby lifeboat. She was the Zoo's first Kodiak bear, and everybody was glad to have her—though no one had the vaguest idea of how to get her from the navy dock to the Zoo grounds. The staff knew nothing about crating an animal of such size, the Zoo had no truck, and there was no money to rent one. So, as Wegeforth later wrote: "We did the only thing we could—put a collar and chain around Caesar's neck and seated her beside Dr. Thompson [one of the Zoo's board members] in the front seat of his auto. As the citizenry gaped, the two of them drove through the city to the Zoo." Thompson smiled nervously, keeping at least one eye on Caesar at all times—needlessly, as it turned out, for the bear was apparently only concerned with enjoying her first ride in an open roadster.

As the Zoo's collection expanded, cages had to be built and new food sources uncovered. With World War I driving prices ever higher, a basic expense such as feeding the animals was a matter for daily anxiety. Early in the morning, before tending to his medical practice, Wegeforth would make the rounds of local produce markets, foraging for damaged fruits and vegetables. On other occasions, he would go down to the waterfront and try to buy a load of fish for less than the wholesale price. He also visited farmers and ranchers in the surrounding countryside, pleading for yet another free load of hay, meat, or animal feed.

Horses, Wegeforth discovered, could serve as both food and income. "Through a curious paradox, the price of hides had risen sharply because of the war but we could purchase horses for practically nothing. So, we fed the meat to the animals and sold the hides for $5 or $6." Another important source of income was lion cubs. "During the first four years of our existence we sold thirty cubs provided us by our obligingly prolific mother lions, at $150 apiece and up, according to their size and condition."

When Wegeforth returned from a stint in the army in January, 1919, he brought with him a single-minded determination to secure a permanent zoo location in Balboa Park. He and others realized that the Zoo could not grow in its original cramped location and they kept pressing the city to provide a larger area for development. Finally, in the fall of 1921, the city's ordinance department approved the present 100-acre site. The city fathers decided that what had formerly been regarded as Wegeforth's folly might now make a notable addition to San Diego's urban design. (Actually, part of Wegeforth's original motive for founding the Zoo had been to help preserve the spaciousness of Balboa Park.)

Today, the Zoo is enveloped in towering trees and lush foliage, but back in 1921 the land turned over by the city was the worst part of Balboa Park, consisting of four arid mesas that were separated from one another by deep canyons. The entire site was covered with cactus and scrub brush, and there were no roads or trails to connect the mesas. Most people felt this rugged acreage was completely unsuited to Wegeforth's purpose, but he, predictably, envisioned a zoo that would capitalize on its unique setting.

"From the first," he later recalled, "I was struck by the marvelous potentialities of the grounds, with mesas and canyons that could be developed into a capacious sylvan zoo . . . I spent my leisure time riding my horse up and down the rabbit trails through the canyons and brush, studying the topography, selecting sites best suited for open grottoes and pools, deciding which animals would be best exhibited on the high, level areas and which would stand the cooler and less protected areas.

"We [also] wanted individual areas for each group of animals. Knowing with what malevolent speed diseases can spread among animals, we wanted these areas some distance apart so that if an epidemic broke out among some of the animals, that area could be isolated and the Zoo would not have to be closed."

To Wegeforth's way of thinking, plants were just as important as animals; he wanted to make the San Diego Zoo a luxuriant zoological *garden* in the fullest sense of the word. He sought to create "a natural woods in which, in irregular and unobtrusive installations, we find rare animals at unexpected intervals, so that, although confined, the sensation thus aroused is comparable to coming upon them in the wild."

With this in mind, Wegeforth devised a network of trails and roads that would make everything accessible to the visitor. He made rough sketches of all that he wanted and had an architect draw up a detailed plan. This plan was approved by the city's park commission and, in early 1922, construction began.

Although the Zoo's location was now legally secure, Wegeforth's financial problems were only just beginning, for, in order to carry out the visionary plans he had for the property, he would have to raise money on a large scale. Deciding to tackle first things first, he visited publishing heiress Ellen Browning Scripps, described his master plan, and asked her to pay for nearly three miles of wire fencing with which to enclose the Zoo grounds. This, once done, would allow the Zoo to collect ten cents for admission. She agreed to pay for the fencing, and later in the year she financed grottoes for bears, lions, and tigers. Her philanthropic support was vitally important to the Zoo during the next ten years, for she underwrote construction of the seal ponds, the magnificent walk-through flight cage which bears her name, and the original

hospital. She also provided funds to acquire many Zoo animals.

Still, with larger grounds, more animals, and a growing staff, ever-increasing amounts of money were necessary. Wegeforth was determined to build fast and to build big, and this, in effect, meant the Zoo was constantly living beyond its means. As one of his friends later remarked, "When you're running a place like this, there are two ways to go. You can live within your budget and stay small, or you can build like crazy and hope to find the money to pay for it somewhere." Harry Wegeforth always chose the latter course. One of his favorite ploys was to borrow money from a bank to begin construction of an exhibit; then, when construction was completed, to casually show the impressive structure to a wealthy person and to point out what a fine gift it would make to the children of San Diego. Early in the fund-raising game, he learned that checkbooks opened more readily once an individ-

Ellen Browning Scripps was a vital financial contributor to the Zoo until her death in 1932.

Interior of the Scripps Flight Cage for shore and wading birds, as it appeared upon completion in 1923

ual had actually seen the structure to be given in his or her name. A similar method was used in the buying of animals, with the added touch that they were frequently named after the intended financial victim.

Another way in which Wegeforth practiced his chicanery was to let a potential donor know that the Zoo's anniversary was coming up and that a gift would help make the occasion an especially memorable one. All went well until several donors got together and realized that the Zoo had had half-a-dozen anniversaries in a single year. When confronted with his duplicity, Wegeforth laughed and insisted that the only way to rectify the situation would be for the donors to write checks for the Zoo's *real* anniversary. Surprisingly, most people did. In fact, many people found themselves donating money, in both large sums and small, simply because they liked Wegeforth and trusted him—and because they admired what he was doing.

"He was a very *kind* man," one of his associates later recalled. "He genuinely liked people and cared about them . . . and they responded in the same way. There was nothing phony about the man, and you could feel that the minute you met him." His patients, his friends, and generations of San Diego children naturally fell into the affectionate habit of calling him "Dr. Harry." People knew that he meant business when it came to the Zoo, and that, whatever else happened, he would never let it fail. He was willing to devote endless hours and most of his own income to the Zoo's cause, and people gave

him money with the complete confidence that it would not be wasted. Wegeforth's likable personality and total commitment did more than just bring money to the Zoo, however; equally important, it attracted other capable people to the effort, convincing them by example to put in long hours for little or no pay. All of these hours of free labor that went into the building and running of the Zoo during its first twenty-five years were crucial to its eventual survival.

"I tried never to lose heart," Wegeforth recalled. "Whenever anybody started to knock my plans, I just kept right on boosting them." According to his biographer, Neil Morgan, very few adversaries could match his tenacity and his skill at marshaling public support. In 1925, when he was battling the city's park commission for control of the Zoo grounds, he enlisted the children of San Diego in his political drive. Printed in the newspapers each day was a sample ballot:

EVERY CHILD'S CHANCE TO VOTE

I want my Zoo kept out of politics and would vote for
    Proposition No. 6 if I could vote on April 7 _____
I don't care what becomes of the elephants and the ponies and the other animals and would vote against
    Proposition No. 6 _____
Name _____
Address _____   *Age* _____
CLIP THIS BALLOT, MARK IT, AND BRING IT WITH YOU TO THE ZOO SATURDAY, WHERE YOU CAN CAST IT IN THE BALLOT BOXES

Harry Wegeforth stands before what was one of the largest cages in the world for birds of prey when it was completed in 1937. The structure has since been expanded and converted into the walk-through Tropical Rain Forest Aviary.

THAT WILL BE PLACED THERE. TELL YOUR FRIENDS AND LET THEM COME AND VOTE TOO. ALL CHILDREN WHO VOTE, WHETHER THEY VOTE YES OR NO, WILL BE GIVEN ICE CREAM AND CAKE FREE, AND MAY ATTEND THE MOVIE SHOW FREE.

Wegeforth's foes howled in protest, charging him with "bribing" the children of the city to influence the outcome of the election, but he turned them aside with the comment, "It is all right to bribe children if the end in view is worthwhile."

Pressured by his dreams and by an ever-increasing overhead, Wegeforth constantly had to search for new ways to raise money. One scheme was a disaster—a "fund-raising" circus that generated a $2,000 loss—yet Wegeforth was indefatigable. When all else failed, and money simply could not be raised

in time, he was not above "liberating" the materials and supplies that he needed. Loads of lumber and stacks of steel rails that had been sitting in the city's supply depot one week, had a way of miraculously reappearing the next—as cages and buildings at the Zoo. On one famous occasion, Wegeforth instructed his maintenance man to tap into the city's water main and to do so without telling the water department. When the man objected, Wegeforth looked surprised. "After all, we're watering half of Balboa Park for the city, aren't we?" The maintenance man could find no flaw in that logic, so he went out and attached a T-joint to the hydrant in front of the Zoo. The ploy went undiscovered for several years.

Other times, Wegeforth seemed almost to *will* good luck his way. A newly completed dam in Alligator Canyon was only partly filled at the Zoo's expense when, Wegeforth recalled, "fortunately for the Zoological Society an automobile crashed into a fireplug and the water ran down the canyon and filled our dam to overflowing."

The Zoo's chronic budget deficit is illustrated by the figures for 1927. In this particular year, the Zoo's two sources of income (the admission charge and a special contribution from the city) amounted to less than $50,000. However, the combined operating and capital improvement costs totaled nearly $135,000. This great discrepancy put a terrific strain on Wegeforth and the other members of the board as they struggled to make up the difference by soliciting private contributions. Finally, in 1934, after four referenda and years of municipal inertia and opposition, the city's yearly contribution was fixed by law—free from political and budgetary pressures—and the Zoological Society was given permanent tax support based upon the assessed value of real property in San Diego. This support helped considerably in the 1930s and 1940s, but as the Zoo expanded, the tax subsidy would eventually cover only the water bill for one year. (Today's operating budget is basically covered by admissions; the sale of food, tours, and gifts; and membership support. Most new construction is funded by donations.)

Through his reading and, later, his worldwide travels, Wegeforth realized that, ultimately, the San Diego Zoo's reputation would rest not on bigger and better enclosures, but on the quality of its animal collection. He approached this goal from several directions, aiming to create a "Zoological Garden with a notable group of animals that could be seen in but few zoos [while] ordinary zoos display the common varieties."

Wegeforth's tight budget forced him into becoming one of the canniest animal traders of his time. One favorite trick was to visit dealers on the East Coast in the fall, when the weather was getting colder and the eastern zoo season was over. He knew full well that dealers would sell at extremely low prices during this time in order to escape the cost of feeding the animals all winter.

Early on, Wegeforth also discovered that many animals common to Southern California, such as California sea lions, pelicans, rattlesnakes, and colorful western kingsnakes were considered rare in many parts of the world and hence much desired by other zoo directors. He turned this to his advantage by using the animals as barter. Mini-expeditions were regularly dispatched to the remote sections of Balboa Park in search of rattlesnakes, and Wegeforth encouraged friends of the Zoo to bring in as many snakes as they could find from the outlying areas of San Diego County. He then converted these reptiles into cash by shipping them to dealers on the Atlantic Coast or by trading them for specimens wanted from other zoos. He did the same with locally caught and readily trained sea lions. As a later director of the Zoo remembers: "Nothing was sold if it could be traded to better advantage . . . and there are many animals in the Zoo that instead of a dollar value should have upon their records a price of one sea lion, five red rattlesnakes, and two sidewinders; or five white pelicans."

In dealing with the wild-animal trade, Wegeforth soon became angered by the tactics of some animal dealers, who, by cornering the market on certain highly desirable species, would run up prices well beyond an animal's real worth. Realizing that zoos could circumvent this situation by trading their surplus animals among themselves, thus bypassing the middleman, Wegeforth contacted other zoo directors and together they formed an organization—today known as the American Association of Zoological Parks and Aquariums (AAZPA)—expressly for this purpose. In addition to providing this basic service, the organization now encompasses a host of equally important duties: fostering professionalism and communication within the zoo world, promoting captive-breeding efforts, and acting as a legislative watchdog in Washington, D.C.

By 1925, thanks to Wegeforth's sharp-witted animal trading, the Zoo's collection was already among the finest in the United States. Most of the animal enclosures were still rather makeshift, and the trails and roads in the park would not be paved for many years to come, but a visitor at this time could see a surprising variety of rare creatures in a few hours' time. There were orangutans from Borneo and Sumatra, wombats from Australia, yaks from Tibet, king vultures from South America, eclectus parrots from the Solomon Islands, the largest group of gibbons outside Asia, and a Malayan sun bear.

Still, Wegeforth envied the Bronx and Chicago zoos their animal-gathering expeditions to Africa and Asia, and he longed to mount his own zoological expeditions to remote areas where rare specimens, capable of making zoological history, might be found. He made his first foray in 1926, returning with huge elephant seals from Guadalupe Island, about 250 miles south

Captain Allan Hancock's yacht, *Velero III,* took Wegeforth on many expeditions to bring back flora and fauna to the Zoo.

of San Diego. His original goal had been to find some Guadalupe fur seals, which, though reportedly extinct, had recently been sighted on the island. The expedition failed to find any fur seals, but the San Diegans left word wherever they landed that they would pay a handsome reward to anyone bringing them a pair of such animals. So, one can easily imagine Wegeforth's astonishment and joy when a fisherman named William Clover appeared at the Zoo on April 25, 1928, with two live Guadalupe fur seals. The following year, Wegeforth wrote: "Our interest in preservation of species leads naturally to our endeavors to discover new species and to throw light on those already known. Our most singular reward for this has been our discovery of the fur seal of Guadalupe Island. There is nothing which has attracted to this Society the attention of scientists and statesmen more than the appearance of these beautiful creatures in our garden has done."

When the stock-market crash precipitated the Great Depression, attendance at the Zoo dropped sharply, donations stopped, and the city council began to question whether the Zoo was a "luxury" San Diegans could afford. Seeing his beloved Zoo threatened with destruction and his private hospital close to bankruptcy, Wegeforth worked even harder to save both ventures, putting in eighteen-hour days, seven days a week. One day, toward the end of 1931, he was completely exhausted and ill with influenza, yet he left his sickbed to repair the crushed elbow of a small girl. In the middle of the operation, he suffered a major heart attack and collapsed.

Wegeforth recovered, but he was forced to abandon his medical practice and was warned to discontinue all strenuous activity and to avoid excitement of any kind. Of course, this advice meant that he would also have to give up the Zoo, but he certainly had no intention of doing that. Starting in 1932, he handed over its day-to-day management to Belle Benchley, his eventual successor, and spent much less time marshaling community support for the Zoological Society. This freed him to travel around the globe at his own expense, gathering animals for the collection. On one such journey, he visited twenty-nine zoos and innumerable animal markets, buying and trading as he went. When he sailed to the Philippines and the Dutch East Indies in 1935, he left San Diego with crates and cages filled with penguins, mountain lions, and sea lions; he returned four months later with orangutans, Philippine turtles, twenty-six gibbons, and a rare blue boar. Yet another cruise took him down the east coast of South America and up the Orinoco and Amazon rivers, where he collected many rare and colorful animals. (When the various ships that would eventually deliver these exotic animals arrived in San Diego, Belle Benchley liked to refer to them as "our ships coming in.")

Despite laboring constantly under a burden of increasingly bad health, Wegeforth's extraordinary efforts between 1932 and 1939 resulted in the addition of more than 1,500 mammals, birds, and reptiles to the Zoo's collection, as well as countless varieties of endangered flora from around the world. But all this would come to an end in 1940, when Wegeforth had to cut short an expedition in India, having fallen ill with a severe case of pneumonia, soon to be complicated by malaria.

Arriving home, he knew he had gone on his last expedition, and for the remaining months of his life, he busied himself by putting his affairs in order and preparing the Zoo's staff and board of directors for the transition that was about to take place. He spent many hours talking with Belle Benchley, acquainting her with the plans he still had for the Zoo's development. When his health permitted, he continued to take a detailed interest in operations and new construction, but as time went by, he was absent from the grounds for longer and longer periods. On June 24, 1941, he asked his friend and assistant, Joe Galvin, to take him to his tailor to be fitted for two new suits. On the following day, he died.

In remembering Dr. Wegeforth, friends recalled the time in 1936 when they decided it was high time he receive some

Elephant seals destined for the Zoo are beached on Guadalupe Island by Hancock's crew.

Wegeforth, standing in the foreground, supervises the capture.

public recognition for his central role in building the San Diego Zoo. They decided to honor him by dedicating a bronze plaque on the new amphitheater (which had been named Wegeforth Bowl). Money was raised, a suitable dedication was composed, and the plaque was affixed to the amphitheater wall—all without his noticing it. At the ceremony, when the plaque was unveiled, Wegeforth stepped forward to scrutinize the wording. Then he turned to his good friends and thanked them—politely. "Well," he said, "it's nice. But you could have bought an animal with the money."

Fourteen years earlier, the Zoo's most important benefactor, Ellen Browning Scripps, had walked into Harry Wegeforth's office and offered to provide him with $5,000 a year to hire a full-time director. She knew that the accelerating growth of the Zoo was making it increasingly difficult for Wegeforth—as president of the board of directors—to supervise the building program, raise funds, manage the day-to-day activities, and keep up with his medical practice. He agreed that it was absolutely necessary to have a qualified person take charge of daily management, but he had been unable to find a man with whom he could work harmoniously—starting with Frank Buck, the animal dealer who was later to gain fame as the star of the "Bring 'Em Back Alive" movies. Yet, in 1925, and without knowing it at the time, Wegeforth was to find the director he so sorely needed.

Belle Benchley (née Jennings) was born on the Kansas prairie in 1882, but her family moved to California when she was still a young girl so that her father could become the sheriff of San Diego County. She eventually earned a teacher's certificate and taught for three years on the Pala Indian Reservation (not far from the present site of the Wild Animal Park), before marrying William Benchley and moving north to Fullerton. When the marriage failed in 1922, she brought her son, Edward, back to San Diego and began studying bookkeeping, one of the few options open to an educated woman at that time. She passed the civil service exam and had applied for a job with the harbor department when Wegeforth hired her as a substitute for the Zoo's vacationing bookkeeper.

Mrs. Benchley was forty-three then, with little business training and absolutely no background in zoology or science, but she so impressed Wegeforth with her natural abilities, her capacity for hard work, and her immediate interest in every aspect of the Zoo that he asked her to stay on once his regular bookkeeper returned.

She had been on the job only three days when a man called asking the length of a hippopotamus's tail. She didn't know whether to laugh or hang up, but she decided to treat the call seriously. (In the years ahead, she was to find that the more peculiar the call, the more likely it was *not* a prank.) She asked the man to hold on and ran outside to look at the hippo's tail. No help there; the animal was underwater. She ran back to the office and rummaged through a pile of zoological magazines and books until she found a scale drawing of a hippopotamus. She measured the animal, subtracting the tail length from the body length, and was surprised to find that the caller was still waiting on the phone. "Thirteen to fourteen inches," she breathlessly said. "Thank you," he said and hung up.

She hardly had time to reflect on the nature of that particular call when others began coming in: "What's wrong with my pet cougar?" "What do hummingbirds eat?" "I have a snake in my bathroom; what kind is it?" Rather than be annoyed, Belle liked to track down the answers to such questions. Each one became a new learning experience, and she was soon acquiring more practical knowledge about wildlife than was in the possession of most academically trained zoologists. She also found that animals were introducing her to another, larger world—one more fulfilling than any she had ever known.

Soon, Wegeforth began turning over many of his duties to Belle. One of these included going to the city to talk about the Zoo and to solicit funds. Although she was initially terrified just thinking about speaking before luncheon clubs and other gatherings, she soon proved her natural aptitude for public relations. She overcame her shyness by using live props from the Zoo, relaxing as she described the particular animal she was holding—what it ate, where it came from, and how it lived in the wild. At the same time, she later recalled, "When I asked a group of prospective donors for money, my appeal was easier and more persuasive if I had a monkey in my arms holding out the tin cup." Even stuffy business leaders would brighten and laugh at the antics of a baby cheetah or a small chimp, and Belle was in her element while fielding questions, reminiscent as this was of her teaching days.

Within two years, Mrs. Benchley had become Wegeforth's indispensable assistant in running the Zoo, and he pressed the board of directors for her appointment as executive secretary of the Zoological Society (whose hierarchy was modeled after the London Zoo's). Taking over this position in 1926, she was, in effect, the director of the Zoo—the first woman ever to hold such a position. She showed, too, that, in her own way, she could be as tough and persistent as Wegeforth. "There was nothing shy about Belle Benchley," said Charles Schroeder, her eventual successor. "If something wasn't going right, or a decision was not being reached, there often came a point when she would almost stamp her foot and say, 'I'm not going to put up with this! I want you to do so-and-so.' "

When it came to animals, however, she was a soft touch. To an animal lover like Harry Wegeforth, one of Belle's most impressive qualities was her instinctive understanding of animals. Back in the 1920s, zoos were primarily concerned with securing animals for display, with no real regard for captive breeding, but Wegeforth knew that every animal successfully reared in captivity was one less he would have to buy, or one more he would be able to trade for other specimens. Belle's interest in Zoo babies was more maternal. She became involved with the fate of each young animal, and over the years she took home dozens of orphans to raise on formulas concocted by the Zoo's hospital staff.

Of all the animals at the Zoo, Mrs. Benchley developed the deepest affection for the apes (those primates without tails), especially the gibbons, orangutans, and gorillas. Her respect for apes was such that when visitors to the Zoo asked her in an obviously deprecating manner whether *she* believed that "man descended" from the apes, she would first explain that that was not at all what Charles Darwin had meant by his theory of evolution, and then remark that "if you compare some people with my apes, you can just leave it at this: 'man descended.' "

One of Mrs. Benchley's most important animal acquisitions, in terms of boosting the San Diego Zoo's worldwide stature, came in 1931 when she secured two male mountain gorillas, Mbongo and Ngagi. They had been captured the year before in the mountains of eastern Zaire by the famous wildlife photographers Martin and Osa Johnson, and had been featured in their film, *Congorilla*. Now they (the gorillas) would become international celebrities, favorites of zoo buffs and scientists alike, who had only recently been able to see and study gorillas in captivity—and few the size of Mbongo (about 120 pounds) and Ngagi (nearly 150 pounds) inside the United States. The

The mountain gorilla Ngagi was reportedly terrified by the turtle held here by former Zoo director Belle Benchley.

gorillas were purchased with a $10,000 check from Ellen Browning Scripps, shortly before she died.

"Mrs. Benchley fell in love with her two gorillas," said Charles Schroeder. "She constantly fed them, even though they were in these fairly small cages and getting little exercise. She'd bring tidbits from home, like raisins and prunes and fruit or a little package of goodies, and she'd sit by their cage and have them come over so she could feed them. We'd tell her, 'The gorillas are overweight; they're becoming obese,' but we couldn't tell her to lay off. Besides, I think she wanted to make them the biggest gorillas anywhere. They were two great animals, but I'm afraid she contributed to their early demise by improperly feeding them." Mbongo eventually grew to be 618 pounds, while Ngagi tipped the scales at 636 in later years.

One reason Mrs. Benchley enjoyed feeding the gorillas so much was because she spent a great deal of her spare time playing with them and cultivating their affection. She made a special effort to develop a friendship with Ngagi, who was older and more aloof than Mbongo. Even so, for months after the gorillas were established in their Zoo quarters, Ngagi remained standoffish. About this time, Belle remarked to a friend, "You don't know what it's like to be snubbed until you've been snubbed by a gorilla."

Then, one day, inside their enclosure, she slid her hand from Mbongo's arm to Ngagi's. The great ape became rigid with fear, and Belle grew half-afraid that he might do her some harm. She softly spoke his name, and when Ngagi turned to look at her, Belle saw that "his big, black face was covered with beads of sweat, and I realized how much greater had been his victory than mine and how difficult it had been to overcome his reluctance to human touch."

When Mbongo died of San Joaquin Valley fever (coccidioidomycosis) in 1942, a sorrowful Mrs. Benchley found time every day to visit the lonely Ngagi, and they would sit holding one another through the bars, consoling each other in their mutual grief. Ngagi died nearly two years later from a blood clot. Today, donated busts of Mbongo and Ngagi are still to be found near the main entrance and are among the most photographed subjects in the Zoo.

Paradoxically, the Depression which had threatened to close down the Zoo in the early 1930s proved to be a blessing when the economy began to revive. Wegeforth applied for aid from

Benchley's eventual successor, Dr. Charles Schroeder, accompanied several expeditions to bring back elephant seals when he was serving as the Zoo's veterinarian in the 1930s.

the Works Progress Administration (WPA) and the resulting outpouring of federal funds enabled him (and Belle Benchley) to turn the Zoo into a monument to public works. From the beginning of WPA assistance until the time it reached its peak, the Zoo's budget for new building, planting, and grounds maintenance was quadrupled, and more than two hundred extra workers were set to work renovating, cleaning, planting, constructing and, in general, completely transforming the Zoo. At first, the WPA provided only labor, but Wegeforth proved that his skill as a scrounger was unimpaired. One day, he was caught supervising the unloading of lumber from a truck at the Zoo. Each board was marked on the end with the initials WPA. When this was called to his attention, the doctor smiled disarmingly. "Oh," he said, "that stands for White Pine, A-grade," and went right on with the unloading. A year or so later, however, this particular subterfuge was no longer necessary, for the WPA began supplying materials as well as labor, and "White Pine, A-grade" was being delivered to the Zoo free of charge.

As a result of the growth of the collection, the beautification of the grounds, and the modernization of the exhibits, Mrs. Benchley inherited a thriving operation when Harry Wegeforth died in 1941. She steered the Zoo through the traumatic months following Pearl Harbor—when preparations were made to help defend the public from the animals in case of a Japanese air attack—and saw attendance soar in the postwar era as San Diego, by that time a major naval port and military training area, continued to grow in population.

When she turned seventy in 1952, Mrs. Benchley gave the board of directors an ultimatum: "If you ever expect me to retire, you must hire Charles Schroeder as my replacement." Her choice of successor was as prescient as Harry Wegeforth's had been years earlier, for Schroeder had the farsighted instincts, the personal toughness, and the charisma needed to bring the Zoo into the modern age of promotion and captive breeding. Short and bouncy, Schroeder was a ceaselessly energetic, ever-cheerful personality who, over the next twenty years, would effect important improvements at the Zoo while masterminding the development of the San Diego Wild Animal Park.

A native of New York City, with a veterinary degree from Washington State University, Schroeder was hired as the Zoo's veterinarian in 1932. As was typical in those hard-pressed days,

he performed many jobs, becoming somewhat of a one-man hospital. "All I had was a secretary, a janitor, and volunteer technicians," Schroeder recalled. "I was the intern, the parasitologist, the microbiologist, the pathologist—and the Zoo photographer." He would go out with his Graflex camera and take pictures of certain prominent animals, then develop the film in a photo lab at the hospital. The next day, his postcards (made from the postcard-size negatives) would be on sale at the Zoo.

As veterinarian, Schroeder initiated an extensive research program delving into the causes of death in zoo animals. Over the next five years, his detailed autopsies and studies of animal physiology, coupled with a rigorous program of hygiene, resulted in a 47-percent reduction in the average annual death rate of animals at the Zoo. Recognizing the value of Schroeder's work, the Bronx Zoo hired him away in 1937, but he returned in 1939 to serve for two years as director of the Zoo hospital.

In his *Gathering of Animals: An Unconventional History of the New York Zoological Society*, William Bridges wrote that Schroeder "certainly rejuvenated the practice of veterinary medicine in the Bronx Zoo. . . . He set up an elaborate record-keeping system, organized a group of distinguished medical men to do research in cooperation with the Animal Hospital, charmed the executive committee into providing money for modern laboratory equipment, and proclaimed as his goal the practice of preventive veterinary medicine, with all that implied in the way of quarantine, close supervision of exhibition quarters, better diet, early recognition of disease, and so on."

Bridges also recounted the following vignette concerning Schroeder: "On Christmas Eve of 1938 a late-working member of the staff passed the Animal Hospital on his way home, saw a light in the rear of the building, and entered to wish Dr. Schroeder a Merry Christmas. He found the veterinarian just outside the back door, a white apparition in the wet snow that had been falling since noon. He had the carcass of a camel suspended from a crane and was doing an autopsy all alone and softly singing 'Stille Nacht, Heilige Nacht.' "

In 1941, Schroeder became a production manager of the Lederle Laboratories in New York (now a division of American Cyanamid), where he supervised development of veterinary uses of sulfanilamides (bacteria-inhibiting drugs) and such antibiotics as penicillin and Aureomycin. However, he still kept in touch with the San Diego Zoo, occasionally acting as Belle Benchley's New York agent. "She'd call and say, 'Charlie, Henry Trefflich [a prominent animal dealer] has a new shipment coming in. Will you take a look for us?' "

When Schroeder came back to San Diego in 1953 to succeed Mrs. Benchley, he had his own philosophy to carry out. Before taking off on a cruise around the world—her retirement gift from the people of San Diego—Belle sensed he was planning to take a different course in managing the Zoo. "She told me one day that I should *never* treat the Zoo like a business," Schroeder recalled. "She said, 'The Zoo is a separate activity— it is not a business.' She truly loved her animals, no question about it, and I loved them too. But I told her, 'No, the Zoo *is* a business and we've got to treat it like one.' We didn't really have words; she just didn't like some of the things I was doing."

One of Schroeder's first decisions was to upgrade staff salaries. He also kept a maintenance crew on duty over the weekend to keep the Zoo clean seven days a week. "Before," he said, "they didn't clean the Zoo from Friday afternoon to Monday morning." As Joan Embery, the Zoo's roving ambassador, wrote in her book, *My Wild World* (coauthored by Denise Demong): "For all the power and pressures of his office, [Schroeder] had a flair for detail. Every evening, he'd walk from one end of the Zoo to the other with a notebook and jot down everything that needed attention, even a trash can that needed to be repaired, an area that hadn't been swept, or a post that was crooked."

Years before, Harry Wegeforth had placed a sign by the front gate announcing that the entire Zoo was "Dedicated To The Children Of San Diego." This sentiment accurately expressed his conviction that a zoo had a purpose far beyond that of entertaining the populace; it had a role to play in educating children about wildlife. It was for this reason that the San Diego Zoo for so long had no admission charge for children and that the education program had always been, and would continue to be, a top priority.

Charles Schroeder carried this philosophy a step further by building a children's zoo within the main grounds. "I got the idea when I was at the Bronx Zoo," he recalled. "Other people opposed it, but eventually they went along." When the Children's Zoo was under construction in 1956–57, Schroeder was positive he knew what could and could not be done with this

Blooming bougainvillea in Benchley Plaza

The sea lion show has been an entertaining staple in Wegeforth Bowl since the late 1930s.

specialized complex, and he was understandably annoyed when a young architectural designer, Chuck Faust, kept insisting that children could be trusted to walk through a cage full of finches without harassing the birds or letting them escape. One thing a veterinarian knows is that people and wild animals do not—and should not—mix. Still, Faust insisted that Schroeder give the walk-through concept a trial. He promised he could design the cage in such a way that, if expectations proved wrong, he could quickly and inexpensively modify it to exclude visitors.

Happily, the walk-through finch cage became a great success, and Schroeder immediately wanted the main Zoo's two existing flight cages to be modified along the same lines. He

Signs at the Zoo offer visual communication that is more than ornamentation.

A Children's Zoo, located within the main Zoo grounds, was one of Charles Schroeder's most popular additions.

Educational programs which stress the interrelationship of mankind with all other species are conducted at both the Zoo and the Park, reaching thousands of children and adults each year. Here, children learn about the guanaco, a relative of the camel, from trainer Kathy Marmack.

School children observe an echidna, or spiny anteater. "The point is to get children interested in the animal world at an early age and to be sure they learn to respect wildlife and regard animals without fear or contempt," said Park educator Sydney Donahoe.

The Tropical Rain Forest Aviary offers a luxuriant hillside home for over fifty species of birds from such places as Australia and Southeast Asia.

asked Chuck Faust to supervise the work. A winding pathway was built through each of the structures, with an exit/entrance at the bottom. This done, people could stroll inside and, while moving from one level to another past lush foliage and splashing waterfalls, see hundreds of birds close at hand, with no intervening barriers. The Zoo's two large flight cages became the first in the world to allow visitors to immerse themselves in a forest or jungle habitat instead of merely to peer into it from the outside. Not about to pass up an idea that was both aesthetic and educational, Schroeder later asked Faust to design a walk-through flight cage for the main entrance at the Wild Animal Park.

One of Charles Schroeder's primary goals when he became director was to develop the Zoo's captive-breeding capabilities. This kind of program was critical, he felt, if the Zoo was to reduce its reliance on dwindling stocks of wildlife and at the same time to protect the future survival of endangered animals. In the early 1950s, zoo directors were already more sensitive to the growing problem of endangered species than were their counterparts in academia, for zoos were having to pay increasingly high prices for many species—with some animals becoming unavailable at any price. By 1959, it was clear to Schroeder that the Zoo would need a much larger facility, away from the city, that could act as a "second campus" for surplus animals and larger breeding groups. His search for land began, but it was not until 1972 that the Wild Animal Park—eighteen times the size of the Zoo—finally opened, securing Schroeder's dream just four months before his retirement.

A permanent stream runs through Cascade Canyon and a winding trail invites exploration.

Nairobi Village

HISTORY OF THE SAN DIEGO WILD ANIMAL PARK

n January, 1971, well over a year before the Wild Animal Park opened to the public, Charles Schroeder received a telegram from Ian Player, the eminent South African conservationist. The cable read: "22 WHITE RHINOS DEPARTED 0600 HOURS 20 JANUARY. LARGEST CONSIGNMENT OF RHINO EVER TO LEAVE SHORES OF SOUTH AFRICA. WE ARE HAPPY THEY ARE GOING TO YOUR RENOWNED ZOO, AND WE WILLINGLY ENTRUST THEM TO YOUR CARE."

At that point, Player's conservation and relocation program had helped save the southern white rhino from extinction, but only a single calf had ever been born in captivity, and this in South Africa. It was hoped that the Wild Animal Park in California could now assist Player's campaign by developing a successfully reproducing captive herd that could in turn populate other zoos around the world.

Victimized by poachers, the southern subspecies of white rhinoceros had dwindled to an estimated twenty specimens in 1929, all of them confined to the Umfolozi Game Reserve in South Africa. Yet, by 1970, as a result of government conservation efforts, their numbers had increased to over a thousand, and several hundred of these had been successfully reintroduced into other reserves and national parks in southern Africa. To avoid overpopulation on the two main reserves, Player started removing over a hundred rhinos each year, using some of this surplus stock to "seed" areas in the wild where the animals had long been absent and offering the rest for export. London's wildlife installation at Whipsnade bought twenty rhinos in 1970 and the Zoological Society of San Diego agreed to a similar purchase, paying a "bulk rate" of $2,800 apiece. (At the time, Player noted that people in some parts of the world were willing to pay up to $100 a pound for ground-up rhino horn, believing it to be an aphrodisiac. This demand had led to severe poaching in unprotected habitats throughout Africa.)

John Fairfield, then head keeper at the Wild Animal Park and a well-regarded zoo professional, was sent to South Africa to observe the rhinos being captured and to return with them as their keeper on the Atlantic crossing to Galveston, Texas. The ensuing rhino saga was to become a memorable part of his life.

"In Pretoria," Fairfield recalled, "I was able to see the first baby rhino born in captivity." [The mother had been pregnant when she was captured.] "Then as we drove into Zululand, I

51

The Wild Animal Park's initial herd of twenty southern white rhinos was captured in South Africa in 1970. Here, Ian Player, then chief conservator for the Natal Parks Game and Fish Preservation Board, loads a rifle with an immobilizing dart.

started seeing adult rhinos floating down the river, dead. Rhinos don't swim and they had drowned in some flooding up-country. That was a pretty disheartening scene, having come all this way to bring rhinos back alive so we could help save them from extinction."

Once captured, the twenty-two rhinos were placed in individual crates for the trip to California (two were actually going only as far as the zoo in San Antonio, Texas). Next, they were taken by truck convoy to the harbor at Durban where they were loaded onto a freighter, out on deck. "Unfortunately," said Fairfield, "we had to wait three days for the ship to finish being loaded, and there was no place to dump the rhino dung. You're talking about animals that weigh between 1,000 and 2,200 pounds and I guarantee you, there's no way you can imagine what it means to have to work around three days worth of rhino dung. It was above my knees and the stench was terrible."

Finally, mercifully, the ship set out to sea, but within two days one of the rhinos bound for San Antonio died and had to be buried at sea. Fairfield feared that he would lose more animals when storms to the north created tremendous swells. "We had very good weather, but our little ship was bouncing around like a champagne cork, which caused a lot of problems for the poor rhinos. They refused to eat, or drink, or even stand up. They liked to lie in specific positions, but they'd lie there so long, the action of the ship caused them to get pressure sores that developed into large abscesses. I had to spend an hour a day treating each animal, which meant day-and-night work. I had to be there constantly or the animal wouldn't make it, so there was almost no time to sleep."

After twenty-five days at sea, Fairfield and his rhinos made it to Galveston—remarkably without the loss of any more rhinos. They traveled in railroad cars to San Diego, and then by truck to the Wild Animal Park. "They looked terrible," Fairfield admitted, "but they were alive and they had a new home."

When the rhinos were released the next day into the South Africa exhibit (a 93-acre enclosure), Fairfield was on top of the crates, opening the doors to let them out. "I felt so good about setting them free, but those crates had been their home for forty-seven days and they were wary about coming out. I had to coax them along from up on top." Yet, once they were outside the crates, the rhinos headed for the nearest water hole, immediately beginning to explore their new surroundings.

Once immobilized, each rhino was loaded into a shipping crate, which was then placed onto a truck with the aid of a winch and rollers.

Actually, they found themselves in an environment that closely resembled their native habitat, and this probably made their adjustment to the Park that much easier. Next came the crucial test: reproduction.

Said Fairfield, "When the realization of all that had taken place sort of sunk in, I was the proudest man around. I doubt that very many people will ever be able to feel that close to any group of wild animals. We were together so long, twenty-four hours a day. I was with them when they were taken out of the wild and put into crates, but I was also the one who let them out, with the thought in mind that maybe they would be more secure as a species by coming to the Wild Animal Park. We always felt that by bringing twenty-two rhinos to the United States, plus the twenty already in England, that if something happened to the main herd in South Africa, we could draw on all our animals in captivity and restart. But I don't think anybody really thought that things would take off the way they did."

Since the males in the new herd were all several years away from breeding maturity, a designated herd sire was brought up from the Zoo. His name was Mandhla and everyone involved was a bit dubious that he would actually be able to carry out his responsibility. Ian Player had shipped Mandhla and a mate to the Zoo in 1962, but in nine years together they had never reproduced, and had never even shown the slightest romantic inclination toward each other. Zoo officials feared that Mandhla was either infertile, too old, or just not interested in

A special truck convoy transported the rhinos from the Umfolozi Game Reserve to the port of Durban, 180 miles away.

The rhinos were loaded aboard a freighter and accompanied across the Atlantic by Park keeper John Fairfield, shown here, and by a member of Ian Player's staff.

Upon their arrival at the Park, the rhinos were released into the South Africa exhibit. Here, Fairfield opens the crate door to let the first rhino out.

breeding, but, as he was the only bull available, he was shipped to the Park in May, 1971. Once he arrived, it became obvious that what he had needed all along was some open space, a herd environment, and the enticement of more than one female. Rhinos are not exactly gregarious animals, but, with the white rhino species in particular, certain socializing needs must be met in order for them to reproduce in captivity.

"Right away, Mandhla started cleaning house," Fairfield recalled. "He delineated his territory by spraying urine and making corner markings of dung, and he turned tough; he would take on whatever came into his territory, whether it was the feed truck, the water truck, or a tractor. Trotting around with his tail straight up in the air and his ears sticking up, he was boss and no one was going to argue with him."

Soon, he had several females pregnant, and the first calf was born in October, 1972. "I can't really describe the thrill I got when I saw this first baby," said Fairfield. "I was the first person to see it, which is a feeling nobody can ever take away. I'm sitting here now with goose bumps, just remembering it." This first offspring was named Zibulo, which is Zulu for "first fruits of man or beast."

Zibulo was the first white rhino born at the Park, in October, 1972.

Since Zibulo's birth, over fifty calves have been born at the Park, proving that the species has successfully adjusted to its California environment.

White rhino silhouetted at sunset

Over the next ten years, Mandhla would sire forty-nine more calves, the largest number of white rhinos born outside of Africa. And if his longtime Zoo mate, Thombazen, was offended, she didn't hold it against him. Sent to the Park herself in September, 1971, she joined his harem and soon became pregnant.

Trying to limit the number in its herd to about twenty animals, the Park has shipped many of Mandhla's offspring to other parts of the world. By exporting most of the babies, generally when they are about a year old, personnel there have averted a possible inbreeding problem, while at the same time helping to stock other zoos and reserves. Meanwhile, Mandhla has remained as herd sire but only as a result of some opportune intervention by Park employees. "Mandhla had definitely been deposed by a younger challenger, Paghati, just as it happens in the wild," said curator Larry Killmar. "He was vocalizing continuously in high-pitched whines and trying to isolate himself, but Paghati would seek him out, give him trouble, then go away. However, we never observed Paghati breeding any of the females nor were we certain he would become a proven breeder, so rather than risk losing Mandhla, Paghati was removed at the first opportunity." Mandhla resumed control of the herd and Paghati found himself shipped off to China as part of an important exchange. (Several years later, when it became important to establish a fresh genetic line, Mandhla had to be sent to a new home, clearing the way for a younger, unrelated herd sire from the historic 1971 shipment.)

Since the early 1970s, the breeding success of white rhinos has been such that they are now off the endangered species list, prompting Jim Dolan, the general curator of mammals, to write in ZOONOOZ (the Zoological Society's monthly magazine): "The remarkable recovery of the southern white rhinoceros from the brink of extinction is a classic example of what can be accomplished—the preservation of a threatened species through the application of modern and enlightened conservation methods." Yet, in his office one day he also cautioned that while "the white rhino's survival in zoos and protected reserves seems assured around the world, many of its natural habitats continue under siege and it has a questionable future surviving in the wild."

The white rhino episode is just one of many tangible successes recorded by the Wild Animal Park as it strives to ensure the future of endangered wildlife. That this effort—and the Park itself—would become a model for other North American zoological facilities was not, however, Charles Schroeder's original goal. Initially (at least publicly), he simply wanted to find a remote piece of land outside the city where the Zoo could house surplus animals and breed larger species, using the resulting offspring to restock the Zoo or to trade with other zoos. But, like Harry Wegeforth many years earlier, once Schroeder sensed the possibilities—and the urgency—of a spacious open-air animal reserve, his vision and determination became indispensable to the creation of such a facility.

"We started a serious land search in 1959," Schroeder recalled, "and numerous areas were explored, until 1962, when we found an 1,800-acre parcel of city-owned land in the San Pasqual Valley [30 miles north of downtown San Diego]. The terrain, rainfall, and temperatures were ideal—typical high veldt of East Africa, rising from 400 to 1,400 feet at the north limits of the property." The project was originally envisioned as sort of a "backcountry zoo" with limited public participation: a simple restroom, a snack bar, and perhaps an overview of some animals to be completed at a total cost of less than $1 million.

"We ended up spending $20 million by the time we opened," Schroeder said, laughing. "And today the place pulls in over one million visitors a year."

Although Schroeder had found what he considered an ideal site, the majority of the Zoological Society's board of trustees were cool to his plans, if not his drive and ceaseless energy. These members saw the Zoo as their primary responsibility; a distant annex in a remote valley far from the population center sounded like financial suicide, and a bit too exclusive for an organization that prided itself on public education and participation. Schroeder's principal supporter on the board, Anderson Borthwick, recalled that it took five separate votes over a period of several years before the project was finally given the go-ahead in June, 1967. "After the fourth vote, one of the trustees said, 'Schroeder, if you bring this up once more, I'm going to vote to fire you.' But Charlie felt there was too much at stake to remain silent and he eventually brought it up again." This time, through attrition on the board and a change in attitudes, he finally won the votes he needed.

An important boost to Schroeder's campaign had come in October, 1966, when the San Diego Zoo hosted a world conference on the role of zoos in wildlife conservation. The remains of Martha, the last known passenger pigeon, who had died in the Cincinnati Zoo in 1914, were exhibited to dramatize the plight of vanishing wildlife and to illustrate the role that zoos could, and should, play in staving off this kind of eventuality. The conference and the exhibit helped convert at least one other board member to Schroeder's point of view. Meanwhile, two feasibility studies conducted by the Stanford Research Institute indicated that a "wild animal park" at the San Pasqual site—to include public viewing of the animals in natural-habitat groupings—would succeed and could be self-supporting.

By 1966, Schroeder already felt that his proposed reserve could serve as both a captive-breeding center and a major source of public education regarding wildlife. That year, as he later wrote, a Site and Planning Committee "picnicked on a large rock outcropping at the backcountry zoo to do a bit of dreaming. It was there that plans for the Wild Animal Park were conceived." The group started having regular picnic meetings at Eagle Peak (just above the site of the present-day bird show), and they envisioned great things for this brush-covered landscape, just as Harry Wegeforth had envisioned great things for Balboa Park fifty years earlier.

After a formal agreement had been reached with the city, in early 1969, groundbreaking ceremonies were held. But one last hurdle remained—a $6-million bond proposal, crucial in terms of providing the necessary funding, had to be approved by San Diego voters in 1970. Dr. Albert Anderson, chairman of the citizens' committee established to fight for the bond campaign, remembered his disappointment when he first viewed the Park site from a jeep driven by Dr. Lester Nelson, then the Zoo's veterinarian. "It was nothing more than a mass of rocks, dirt, and sagebrush. I just knew there was no way of selling this to the citizens of San Diego." Yet he was caught up by Nelson's enthusiasm and by his vision of what the land could become in time. "His hope for the future wiped away any doubt that I had." Voters eventually shared that optimism, approving Proposition B by a comfortable margin and giving Zoo officials an indication of potential public support as well.

With an ambitious Park concept now approved, two goals had to be achieved: (1) the development of a tourist attraction that could eventually become self-supporting and (2) the main-

tenance of a largely self-sustaining collection of animals for both the Zoo and the Park. Schroeder knew that his staff would have to adapt the San Pasqual Valley landscape to the needs of exotic wildlife *and* the needs of the people desiring to see that wildlife, but a way had to be found that would not jeopardize the sense of sanctuary that, for many animals, is essential to sustained breeding success.

After studying a variety of transportation systems that could provide for public viewing of the animals out in the field, a study committee wisely chose an electrically powered monorail. Running silently on rubber wheels, the train has proven comfortable, durable, and nonpolluting. "We had these big expansive valleys surrounded by steep canyon slopes," Schroeder said, "so we wanted to have an elevated monorail bed that would allow for clear vision of all animals below [and on the slopes above]. We didn't know exactly what animals would come to the Park or who would live where, but we knew they would eventually be on exhibit in all these valleys." Soon after the monorail system had been decided upon, Schroeder, architectual designer Chuck Faust, and construction superintendent Hal Barr hiked the proposed five-mile route, using stakes with red flags to mark the trail they wanted.

Expanding on the original concept, Park officials realized that closeup viewing of some of the animals would also be desirable. This led to the creation of Nairobi Village, a 17-acre "port of entry," where various exhibits showing a representative cross section of animals were constructed. Included were the Gorilla Grotto, Tropical America (a walk-through aviary devoted to animal and plant life native to Central and South America), monkey enclosures, exotic waterfowl lagoons, and the Petting Kraal, where visitors could pet and feed exotic deer, antelope, and goats. Eventually, venues were also created for the different entertainment shows featuring elephants, horses, birds of prey, and canines.

Meanwhile, starting in 1969, Jim Dolan began to accumulate the Park's animal collection. He had been assistant curator of birds at the Zoo, but in Schroeder's estimation, "Jim was the most capable guy we had for this job." Dolan grew up in New York City, the son of a police detective, yet he had always wanted to work with animals. "From the time I was a boy," he said, "I never had an interest in doing anything else. My father also liked animals and we spent a lot of

Construction on the monorail
roadbed in December, 1971

Nairobi Village under construction. The unfinished entrance aviary is to the upper right and Simba Station—the terminus for the monorail—is in the center.

Nairobi Village as it appears today

Overleaf:
Chilean flamingos in Nairobi Village

time together at the Bronx Zoo." After graduating from Mount St. Mary's College in Emmitsburg, Maryland, Dolan acquired his Ph.D. in zoology at the University of Kiel—an experience that has since resulted in numerous important animal exchanges with zoos in both West and East Germany. After a stint at the Catskill Game Farm in New York, he began working at the San Diego Zoo in 1963.

Faced with stocking the Park from scratch, Dolan transferred some animals from the Zoo but was continually on the telephone or traveling around the country, visiting zoos, reserves, and animal dealers in an attempt to acquire the rest. Once the animals arrived, they were housed in holding pens until the various exhibits were completed.

"We concentrated heavily on acquiring hoofed stock, especially endangered species, because the Park's terrain and climate is geared to that type of animal," said Dolan. "We also designed exhibits that were large enough to allow for the formation of herds of up to sixty or seventy individuals in a gregarious species." As he wrote in ZOONOOZ: "The old zoo concepts for managing large animal species had to be put aside and new methods for their husbandry undertaken if long-term, self-sustaining populations were to be established as safeguards

An aerial overview of the Park's field exhibits, which are encircled by the monorail

A herd of axis deer stand in front of the monorail in their Asian Plains exhibit.

against extinction. Such a goal could not hope to achieve the necessary success where only two or three individuals of a given species could be accommodated. Genetic diversity would be greatly reduced, which could ultimately lead to the collapse of the entire project."

Rick Cuzzone, a keeper from the Zoo, and his wife, Shirley, were the Wild Animal Park's first residents. They moved the Zoo's mobile home there on August 5, 1969, and the first exotic animal—a male nilgai (a member of the antelope family)—arrived in September. Other early arrivals included Uganda kob, greater kudu, gemsbok, sable antelope, and Grevy's zebras. The first animal born at the Park was a Formosan sika deer named Alpha, on June 25, 1970.

"After the rhino shipment arrived [in early 1971]," wrote Cuzzone in ZOONOOZ, "the exotic animal population explosion really started. We speculated as to what the poor native rabbits, rattlesnakes, and coyotes must have thought as their homes were invaded by rhinos, zebras, gnus, and high-jump-

ing springboks." The Cuzzones even had a female pronghorn as their alarm clock. At daylight, she would scratch on the door to let them know she wanted breakfast. She and her mate would also follow Cuzzone on his patrols inside the Park, running alongside his jeep at speeds of up to 25 miles per hour.

When the Wild Animal Park was formally dedicated on May 9, 1972, the overall commitment was expressed in this official theme:

Join us here . . .
. . . to contemplate the wild animals of the world and nature's wilderness
. . . to strengthen a commitment to wildlife conservation throughout the world
. . . and to strive toward Man's own survival through the preservation of nature.

South Africa's Ian Player, for so many years the white rhino's most important ally, was a special guest speaker on that

The Uganda kob, a medium-sized antelope, is strongly but gracefully built. Habitat destruction and political turmoil throughout Uganda have drastically reduced its numbers in the wild.

The greater kudu, second-largest of the antelope species, stands over five feet high at the shoulder.

day and he added these inspirational thoughts: "I am a religious man—but my religion is the religion of the wilderness. When I stand here and look out across the valley to the hills, and to those elephants we see standing there, I think of all the people who will be visiting this Wild Animal Park at San Pasqual. For as long as civilized man remains here in the state of California, some people will come for spiritual uplift."

The elephants that Player saw from the podium were six young female African elephants who had arrived earlier in the year as a gift from the Rhodesian government. They all resembled little Dumbos with their huge, floppy ears, and in the ensuing years would provide a fascinating challenge to the Park as it sought to develop a viable reproducing family unit. (Although there are still nearly a million African elephants alive today, they are listed as an endangered species. Some wildlife experts, including Jim Dolan, believe they are doomed in the wild and must be successfully bred in captivity if eventual extinction is to be avoided.)

A crucial step in the African elephant project came in 1977 when Dolan secured Chico as a herd bull for the females. Wild-caught in Zambia, Chico had lived in Spain and then at the Riverbanks Zoological Park in Columbia, South Carolina, where he had worn out his welcome by breaking down the door to the elephant barn and, later, by reaching out and snaring the zoo director with his trunk. Chico was offered to Dolan, who quickly agreed to take the gamble involved, since he had a much larger enclosure to work with and breeding males from the wild were virtually impossible to secure.

Chico was approximately twelve years old when he arrived at the Park and his adjustment was not an easy one. Explains Dolan, "In the wild, African bulls are driven out of the herd at about this age because the whole setup is matriarchal. So Chico had to establish his dominance. He got into a few nasty scuffles and Peaches, the oldest cow, whacked him on the head and spread-eagled him once. But in time he grew to be the largest animal in the group, which gave him pretty good control of the situation."

By late 1979, Chico had his own separate exercise yard and a barn where he was brought in at night. "We left him out with the cows during the day," said head elephant keeper Gary Miller. "Then, when he'd pick out a cow who was in estrus, I'd isolate them in his yard and he'd mate with her ten to twenty times over a period of three days." Chico impregnated

South African sable antelope are beautiful but pugnacious. In the wild, lions are their only true predators.

A pair of Grevy's zebras drink from a pond in the East Africa exhibit, where they lived until they were moved to their own hillside area. Grevy's are the largest of the zebras and, like their relatives, are poached for their skins.

Chico, the African elephant bull, out for a romp in his enclosure

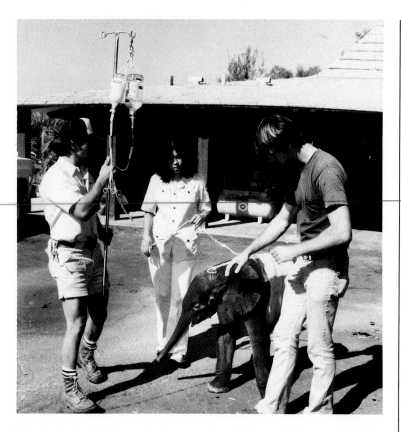

Thor, the first African elephant ever born in California, shown exercising following surgery to repair internal damage caused by a goring from which he did not recover

mother, or try to hand-rear him. Nobody had ever hand-raised an African elephant in the Western Hemisphere from day one, and we didn't feel confident that we could milk the mother often enough or long enough to give him the nourishment he needed."

So Miller went out into the main elephant enclosure with Deteema and Thor, acting as a protective "nanny" for this initial introduction. "We felt that we had to give it a try, and if it didn't work, *then* we would hand-rear Thor the best we could. Everything went well for about ninety minutes as Thor sort of explored the enclosure, with Deteema close by. Some of the cows would run by, smell Thor, and then run off. A couple of the others actually punched him and touched him with their trunks, as if to say, 'What are you? What are you made out of?' which is understandable, since they had never seen a baby before."

When Thor tired, Miller got ready to lead him back to the barn. "Deteema had her back to the herd as it went by for the last time, checking Thor out, and I was about 20 feet away, thinking everything was going to be okay. But Sharpi [a 7,000-pound expectant mother] lagged behind. I watched her and suddenly she balled her trunk up and I thought, 'Uh, oh, trouble,' and I started screaming and running right at her. She saw me coming but she knew what she felt she had to do: she just ran up and did a headstand on Thor, thrusting three or four times with her tusks. Then she ran off."

While Miller chased Deteema away for safety reasons, two other keepers ran in to pick up Thor and guide him into the barn. Sharpi's tusks had penetrated both walls of Thor's large intestine, forcing Park veterinarians to remove eight inches of intestine in an eight-hour operation. The operation was termed a technical success, and ten Park attendants began massaging and patting Thor to stimulate him as the anesthesia wore off. Within an hour, he was back on his feet and making noise again, raising hopes that he might survive. Six hours later, however, he died of respiratory failure.

When news of Thor's death spread, the Zoo and Park switchboards were jammed with phone calls from people wondering why Thor had been put into the herd in the first place, and why, if it had to be done, he had been placed there at such an early age. Dolan pointed out that every effort had been made to integrate Thor safely into the herd and that the Park had good reason to believe it would be a success and in the

five of the females within a year, and then the life-and-death dramas began.

On August 22, 1981, Deteema gave birth to Thor—the first elephant born in California. Named after the Norse god of thunder because of the frequent trumpeting sounds he made as an infant, Thor weighed just over 200 pounds and stood about four feet tall. He soon caught the public's fancy, with his picture appearing in newspapers from coast to coast and his ear-flapping, trunk-hugging antics recorded by the television network news. But alas, the jubilation at the Park was short-lived.

Nine days after his birth, it was decided that Thor and his mother should be released into the main herd. "We had no real option," said Gary Miller. "Deteema was determined to be out with the main herd during the day, and the gates in our elephant barn were not strong enough to hold her. So, we either had to take our chances by letting Thor out with his

Although Sharpi attacked Thor when he was released into the elephant yard, she proved to be an excellent mother with her own Tavi.

Tavi with four adult elephants,
in Chico's bull pen

baby's best interest. He explained, for instance, that elephant mothers often grow nervous and refuse to suckle their calves if taken from the herd. He also conjectured that Sharpi probably attacked Thor because she was frightened by this unusual little creature.

The only benefit gained from this tragedy was a better understanding of what to expect when the next elephant was born, especially since the expectant mother was Sharpi. Talking beforehand, the now-retired Park veterinarian Lester Nelson said, "If Sharpi drops her calf and decides she doesn't like it—and immediately turns around and gores it—then there isn't anything we can do about it. We're certainly not going to send a keeper in there with her to try to protect the baby. We can keep a twenty-four-hour watch on the mother and the baby, like we did with Deteema and Thor, but Sharpi's birth could be just as traumatic in the end."

Before Sharpi delivered (in late January, 1982) Park personnel took some important precautionary steps. First, they trimmed Sharpi's tusks back, which meant they would come in thicker and heavier—but less lethal—when they grew back. Second, they reinforced the doors inside the elephant barn, so that individual animals could be controlled inside. "We didn't think that was a problem," said Miller, "until Deteema crashed through both existing doors one morning in order to join the main herd; she was going, with or without her baby." Third, Chico's isolation yard was modified to serve as a temporary maternity pen for the mother and her baby, thus allowing them to be outside and at the same time to be separated from the main herd. And fourth, keepers began spending more time handling the African elephants instead of simply maintaining them.

"The elephants had all been given some basic obedience training, like lifting their feet so we could chain them up at night, but personal contact was missing," said Miller. "So, we started working on disciplinary things, such as picking up a foot and just holding it there so we could trim it. This is an important form of control over the animal. If they tolerate this, then you can get them to cooperate on something else. We also had each elephant get used to staying inside the barn by herself for a couple of hours every day, so she wouldn't get quite as upset about being left behind when she had a baby." (In addition to Sharpi, three other females were pregnant at the time.)

Fortunately, the fears about Sharpi were all for naught. When she gave birth to Tavi she proved to be an excellent mother, nursing regularly and forming a healthy bond with her offspring. Initially, they were kept inside the barn in the morning and then let out on exhibit for about four hours in Chico's enclosure while he was locked up. Much later, the mother and calf would be integrated into the main herd. "Sharpi is a much more dominant female than Deteema," noted one keeper. "She will protect her baby when they go out with the others." In the interim, a pregnant female named Mandavu (and another elephant, Sabu) kept Sharpi and Tavi company in Chico's enclosure.

When Mandavu gave birth, there were difficulties from the beginning. Her baby, Kumi, was unusually large (287 pounds) and she had problems delivering him through the birth canal. Kumi himself was weak on his feet and unable to hold his head and trunk up to nurse. Mandavu did her best, trying to assist Kumi by holding his head up with her feet and trunk, but as nursing did not take place the maternal bond weakened and she soon lost interest in the baby. Keepers attempted to hand-feed Kumi, but he developed an allergy to both his mother's milk and to infant formula. He lost weight steadily after developing a kidney problem and other ailments and, after a month, had to be euthanized because he was suffering and there was no chance that he would survive.

Before Kumi died, however, Wanki gave birth to Margo, and the two formed a healthy bond. A third successful birth soon followed, this time to Hatari (who was featured in the 1969 movie by that name starring John Wayne). Hatari and her baby, Tsavo—the only surviving male of the five elephants born in 1982—joined the other mothers and babies, and this time all were released into the main herd without incident.

The Wild Animal Park now has a similar breeding program underway with the Asian elephants, featuring a bull named Ranchipur and eight females. Bracing for the expected population explosion, officials are now planning a new $400,000 Asian elephant barn that will include ample maternity pens and several introduction yards that will be used to ease the offsprings' integration into the main herd.

An ultimate goal in the propagation of endangered species—at any zoological institution—is to place them back into their natural habitat someday. This return to the wild may be

Margo, the fourth calf born at the Park, follows her mother, Wanki.

Keepers help Hatari nurse her newborn calf, Tsavo.

Tavi, Margo, and Tsavo enjoy playing in the water.

Tsavo is framed by Hatari, who as a youngster co-starred in a John Wayne movie bearing her name.

Viewed from the side, the horns of the Arabian oryx blend into one, leading some historians to speculate that this animal was the model for the fabled unicorn.

a questionable dream for many animals (including those who gain endangered status in the coming years), given the casualties inflicted by political and military turmoil, poaching, and the ever-increasing, worldwide encroachment upon wilderness environments. Yet, the Arabian oryx does offer a full-circle conservation story, illustrating, too, the effectiveness of the Wild Animal Park as it helped this treasured animal go from virtual extinction, to successful propagation in captivity, to reintroduction back into its native habitat. The oryx odyssey is also an example of how zoos, conservation groups, and governments must work together on an international level in order to save endangered species from extinction.

The oryx (pronounced or-ix) is a beautiful sand-colored antelope with two long, straight horns. (When viewed from the side, the two horns sometimes appear as one, leading historians to believe that this animal was the model for the fabled

Arabian oryx with two calves. About thirty oryx now live at the Park, most of them in a hillside area opposite the Asian Plains exhibit.

unicorn.) Said Jim Dolan, "Arab tradition held that if a hunter killed an oryx, eating the animal would give him great stamina for the rest of his life. Tribesmen would hunt them on foot and from camelback, using spears and bows and arrows, and an individual might only kill one or two in a lifetime, so this really wasn't a threat to the oryx' survival. But after World War II, people began to hunt them for sport using submachine guns and high-powered rifles." By 1972, an animal that once roamed the deserts of the Middle East was all but extinct.

The first fortunate step toward their ultimate survival came in 1962, when the Fauna Preservation Society of London and the World Wildlife Fund mounted an expedition called Op-

Former Park veterinarian Dr. Lester Nelson checking an oryx before it was crated and shipped to Jordan in 1978. The animal's horns are protected by rubber tubing.

One of San Diego's oryx reintroduced to its native habitat at the Shaumari Wildlife Reserve in Jordan

eration Oryx to rescue those few still remaining in the wild. Eventually, the expedition managed to bring back three adult animals—two bulls and one cow—delivering them to the Phoenix Zoo (selected because it offered a climatically suitable home). Within a year, those three animals were joined by six others, donated by the London Zoo and the rulers of Kuwait and Saudi Arabia. (The Shikar-Safari Club International had put up the money to transport the animals to their new home and to build their housing facilities.)

These nine oryx at the Phoenix Zoo formed the nucleus of the first captive breeding group of Arabian oryx and were called the "World Herd." Placed together like this in one location, the oryx proved to be prolific breeders, and when second-generation offspring gave birth, this seemed to insure their ultimate survival as a species—at least in captivity.

The next crucial step was to disperse the World Herd, not only to minimize the potential dangers of inbreeding, but to protect against the loss of the entire herd through a fast-spreading disease or illness. Dispersal of the large Phoenix herd began in November, 1972, when six animals were transferred to the Wild Animal Park. Over the next ten years, ninety-one babies were born at the Park while other breeding groups were started at the San Diego Zoo; the Los Angeles Zoo; the Gladys Porter Zoo in Brownsville, Texas; Tierpark Berlin; and zoos in Zurich and Rotterdam.

Equally important—certainly in a symbolic sense—the oryx were being returned to reserves in the Middle East. In February, 1978, the Wild Animal Park shipped four males to the Shaumari Wildlife Reserve in Jordan, a 5,500-acre tract of land in the Syrian Desert. Fari, the Park's first male offspring, was included in this initial group. A herd of female oryx later joined their male counterparts, and they have since produced eight offspring.

Other shipments to the Middle East followed, including one to Jiddat al Harāsĭs, a vast stony plateau in the heart of Oman where the last wild Arabian oryx were known to have existed. The animals were temporarily housed in a one-third-square-mile pen, but eventually released onto the 19,305-square-mile jiddat which has distinct natural boundaries but no perimeter fencing. Although an offspring was born to the first group of animals to arrive in Oman, their reintroduction into the wild was not without peril: shortly after arriving, one adult male died from a sand viper snakebite. As Dr. Mark Stanley-Price, a manager for the Omani Project, acknowledged, "It may take a couple of years for the oryx to adapt completely to their species' homeland, to learn to forage for food on their own, and to become wild again." In the interim, each member of the original herd has been fitted with a small radio collar so that its movements can be followed and its progress monitored.

By the end of 1981, there were an estimated four hundred Arabian oryx alive in the world (not including those animals which comprised the original World Herd), with captive herds existing in Israel, Morocco, Qatar, and several private locations on the Arabian Peninsula. "We have three breeding groups going ourselves—two at the Park and one at the Zoo," said Jim Dolan. "So we can cross bloodlines, ship animals out, and bring others in. By exchanging and sending additional animals around the world, we can prevent inbreeding in small herds. We've sent a group of four to St. Catherines Island in Georgia [the New York Zoological Society's facility] to start another herd there. So Operation Oryx is on its way. The animal needs to be watched, but we can shut the red light off." He also added, "It is gratifying to know that with each shipment of Arabian oryx to the Middle East and their successful reintroduction there, we are getting closer to the day when herds of the oryx may be seen grazing undisturbed."

A GORILLA FAMILY SAGA —
FROM ALBERT TO JITU

arly in August, 1949, Charles Schroeder was working at Lederle Laboratories in New York when Belle Benchley called him with a special request. Could he examine three baby gorillas that were being held in Henry Trefflich's animal compound in Manhattan, and advise her about their possible purchase? Trefflich had warned her that the gorillas were sick and so tiny that they required round-the-clock care. But once Schroeder had given his medical approval, Mrs. Benchley willingly took the gamble, for here was an opportunity to become the first zoo in the world to raise three young gorillas together. Moreover, the Zoo's gorilla cage had been empty since the death of Kenya in 1947, and more than $5,000 had been built into a public fund with the express intent that the money be used toward the purchase of gorillas.

Fortified with antibiotics to combat their respiratory ailments, the three babies were flown to San Diego with Sadie Taylor, Trefflich's longtime aide. These were lowland gorillas from the French Cameroons, so it was decided they should be given African place-names: Albert (the male), Bata, and Bouba. Weighing just eight pounds, Albert was the runt of the litter,

barely able to sit up alone. He was the youngest, too (about four to six months old), but as his "sisters" were also young enough to require nursing from a bottle and baby food, they were all basically treated like human infants.

Since the gorillas obviously required full-time attention, the job was offered to Edalee Orcutt Harwell, a secretary to the Zoo vets who had already had some experience in working with animals at the hospital and in the holding areas. As she would later recall in ZOONOOZ: "There was no Children's Zoo nursery in those days, so the three babies lived upstairs in the Zoo hospital, in a room provided with cribs. When they outgrew the cribs, they moved to a sunny corner room with individual sleeping cages and a large fenced play area, with bars for climbing. An enclosure was also constructed behind the hospital which held tire swings, ropes, a teeter-totter, and a metal slide. The young gorillas delighted in charging up the slide, stamping their feet to make all the noise possible. Otherwise their play was very quiet. . . . Occasional disagreements brought warning 'coughs' or earsplitting screams that seemed impossible coming from such small individuals. Best of all was when they could get their human friends to swing

Former director Belle Benchley holds Albert, Bouba, and Bata upon their arrival at the Zoo in August, 1949.

The three young gorillas, Bata, Bouba, and Albert

them by the hand, to chase them, or tickle them. The low chortling laugh from being tickled went on and on like a small, raspy engine."

Once the gorillas outgrew baby bottles and cereal, they were taught to eat like people, sitting up in chairs and using cups, spoons, and bowls. This learning process not only made life interesting, it also helped to establish important habits—habits that would come in handy whenever medication had to be administered. "With a sweet orange-flavored vitamin syrup as an incentive," recalled Harwell, "Albert soon learned to handle a spoon by himself, and all three later ate their mush and baby food using a spoon and bowl. They drank their milk and juice from cups. This made it easier when runny noses or upset tummies required medication. They were protected as much as possible from the infant diseases of civilization and all had their sugar cubes with polio vaccine."

As the gorillas grew older, they were driven over to the gorilla exhibit cage on weekends and allowed to spend a couple of hours playing and entertaining the public. This was done

Attendant Edalee Orcutt Harwell observes Bouba feeding
herself with a spoon.

GORILLA FAMILY TREE

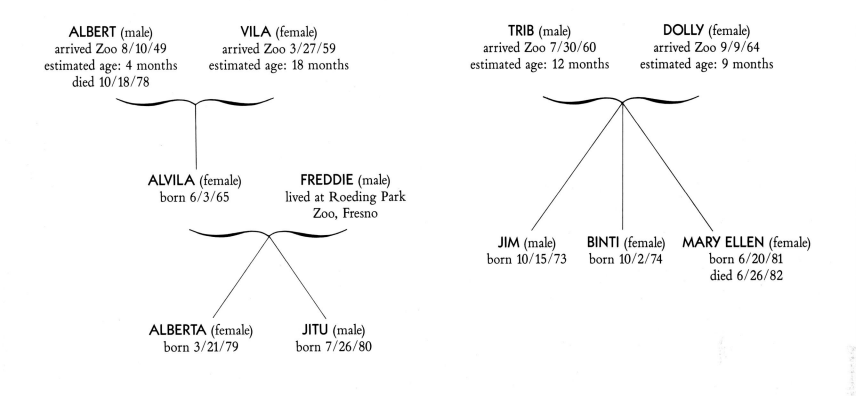

ALBERT (male)
arrived Zoo 8/10/49
estimated age: 4 months
died 10/18/78

VILA (female)
arrived Zoo 3/27/59
estimated age: 18 months

TRIB (male)
arrived Zoo 7/30/60
estimated age: 12 months

DOLLY (female)
arrived Zoo 9/9/64
estimated age: 9 months

ALVILA (female)
born 6/3/65

FREDDIE (male)
lived at Roeding Park
Zoo, Fresno

JIM (male)
born 10/15/73

BINTI (female)
born 10/2/74

MARY ELLEN (female)
born 6/20/81
died 6/26/82

ALBERTA (female)
born 3/21/79

JITU (male)
born 7/26/80

in order to prepare them for the day when, having outgrown their hospital home, they would have to be moved to the Zoo grounds. (Such was their appeal that on the very first day they went on public display, they drew a record crowd of over ten thousand people.) Built originally for the giant mountain gorillas, Ngagi and Mbongo, who died in the early 1940s, the cage was quite high but Albert seemed to enjoy scaring everybody by climbing to the top of it and hanging there by a hand or a foot. Bata, meanwhile, showed an uncharacteristic affinity for water. "She loved to be squirted with a hose," said Harwell, "and she enjoyed sitting in the shallow drinking pool and splashing around." The gorillas were also given a large wooden ball to play with—until they started lifting the ball and banging it into the bars.

After taking up residence in the exhibit cage, the Zoo's gorilla trio continued to live there until an open-air grotto was completed in 1963. The move to these new quarters, coupled with the troop's emerging sexual maturity, prompted several important changes as the Zoo sought to develop a reproducing

family unit. Although the gorillas had been captured in different areas of the Cameroons, they had grown up as brother and sister instead of as potential mates. So Bata, the least compatible of the three, was sent to the zoo in Fort Worth, Texas. Then, Albert and Bouba were joined by Vila and Trib, two young graduates from the Children's Zoo.

Vila, who had been wild-captured as an infant, was about seven years old when she was introduced to the family group in 1964. Albert and Bouba had never mated, so it was up to Vila to bring out Albert's amorous side and keep his family line going. This she did, and on June 3, 1965, Albert and Vila became the parents of Alvila—only the seventh gorilla ever to be born in captivity. Even before this historic birth, Albert had grown into a majestic silver-backed adult and a major celebrity in the zoo world. Now, the congratulatory telegrams poured in, in numbers far exceeding those recorded for any previous birth at the San Diego Zoo.

Although Alvila would be Albert's only offspring (he died in 1978), he nevertheless provided an indispensable example to

all the other males living in his troop. "Albert was nothing to brag about as a breeder," noted Gale Foland, one of his keepers. "In fact, we were lucky to get one kid out of him, because he just wasn't all that interested in the females. However, in all fairness, he had nobody for a role model as he grew up, and he provided that model for all the different males who later came through here, like Trib, Mimbo, and Junior. They had an adult male to emulate and a family to fit into." One episode that clearly illustrates Albert's leadership qualities came in 1969 when the Skyfari opened. At that time there were about six gorillas in Albert's troop and they were all out on exhibit when the first Skyfari car passed overhead. Albert saw it and immediately herded the gorillas underneath for cover. He then stood guard, carefully studying each car as it passed by. He kept his troop there for nearly an hour until he was satisfied that the cars posed no threat.

Once two gorillas mate successfully in captivity, the next crucial question becomes whether the female will respond appropriately as a mother. In the wild, a female gorilla will watch brothers and sisters being born and cared for, and as she grows older she will baby-sit, learning to hold a baby and to carry it around on her back. In captivity, however, unless she has been reared in a family troop and thus afforded the opportunity of witnessing the mothering process, she will have no idea of what to do with a baby. "Females in this situation are highly nervous to begin with," said Sue Kennedy, the keeper in charge of gorillas at the Wild Animal Park, "and they're thoroughly confused by this strange little furry bundle. In almost all cases, either they simply walk away and reject the baby, or they try to hold the baby but never manage to get it close enough to their breast to nurse." When this occurs, the baby must be pulled for hand-raising by humans, a process that takes at least a year, and sometimes longer.

Vila (Albert's mate) and her daughter Alvila offer a good example of the way in which the problem can often be perpetuated from one generation to the next until a self-sustaining troop is established. Raised in the Children's Zoo nursery until her introduction to Albert in the Zoo's Gorilla Grotto, Vila didn't know what it meant to be a mother. When she gave birth to Alvila, she tried to stuff the baby back inside, and instead of cradling her, she held her upside down and even dropped her several times. Thus, Alvila had to be raised in the

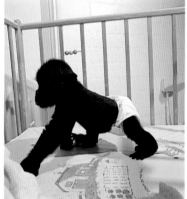

Albert as a majestic silver-backed adult. The term "silver-backed" is used to denote maturity in male lowland gorillas, who, at the age of twelve to fourteen, begin to develop a silver saddle on their backs and legs. Bushy arms and a large sagittal crest are also signs of male maturity.

Alvila, the first gorilla born at the Zoo, had to be hand-raised in the Zoo's nursery when it became clear that her mother, Vila, did not know how to take care of her.

By 1982, Alvila had matured into an adult with two off-spring to her credit, Alberta and Jitu.

Zoo nursery for three years. In 1972, she and Massa, a wild-caught gorilla from Africa, were among the first residents at the Wild Animal Park's large new gorilla facility, but the pairing failed when they developed a sibling, rather than a mating, relationship. As a result, Alvila was sent on breeding loan to the Roeding Park Zoo in Fresno, where she was paired with Freddie.

This maneuvering paid off, for a year later, in March, 1979, Alberta arrived—a rare second-generation birth in captivity. Unfortunately, Alvila was unprepared for motherhood and after six days it became apparent that Alberta was suffering from weakness and lack of nourishment. She then had to be hand-raised in Fresno for three weeks until she was strong enough to make the trip to the Wild Animal Park. (According to the breeding-loan agreement, this first offspring belonged to the Zoological Society of San Diego.)

Once there, another problem common to hand-raising had to be tackled; namely, the introduction of a people-oriented

When Alberta joined the Park's gorilla troop after being raised in the Animal Care Center, she counted on her grandmother, Vila, for comfort and protection.

Trib, the silver-backed troop leader at the Park

gorilla to a troop of gorillas. This is a time-consuming process that can't be rushed along, and in Alberta's case it took almost two years.

When she was about two months old, Animal Care Center personnel began taking steps to ease her eventual transfer to the family group, which consisted of Trib, the silver-backed male; Vila; Dolly, Trib's favored mate; and two juveniles, Jim and Binti, who were Trib and Dolly's offspring. The keepers took Alberta on regular visits to the off-exhibit bedrooms, where she could get used to the sights, sounds, and smells of other gorillas. Still, the actual introduction process, starting when Alberta was one-and-a-half years old, was rather terrifying, even though she was initially placed with Vila, her gentle maternal grandmother. Vila had originally been transferred from the Zoo to mate with Trib, but she would now fulfill what was possibly an even more important role—that of intermediary between Alberta and the rest of the family troop. As Sue Kennedy recalled:

Alberta was frightened when we first locked her into the cage with Vila. It was like putting a child in with a gorilla. But we had no other choice. After one-and-a-half years of nurturing by people, she had to learn how to be a gorilla. Vila was very calm with her, but it still took more than a month before Alberta would go over and sit with her and allow Vila to touch her. Once she established that rapport with Vila, and she had an ally who accepted her and would protect her, then we could start introducing her to everybody else, one at a time. We couldn't just throw her in with the entire troop because there was no telling what they would do.

Trib and his first offspring, Jim, scurry across the exhibit.

Behaviorist Steve Joines used this stuffed doll to help prepare Dolly, Trib's favored mate, to care for her own baby, after she failed to show maternal concern for her first offspring.

The first day Alberta was out on exhibit with the troop, Vila was worried about her falling in the moat [a 10-to-15-foot drop to cement] and she literally went over and picked her up every time she got too close to the edge. That's when they started holding and hugging each other and Alberta began riding on Vila's back. From then on, it was a good situation. Alberta stuck with Vila and followed her everywhere. If she got into a squabble with one of the juveniles, Jim or Binti, she would either rush over to Vila for protection or Vila would come to her aid.

Before Alberta arrived at the Park, Dolly herself had gone through an intriguing training program in how to become a successful mother. Captured in the wild as an infant and then hand-raised at the San Diego Zoo, Dolly was moved to the Wild Animal Park in 1972. She mated with Trib and gave birth to Jim in 1973, but he had to be removed to the Animal Care Center when Dolly showed that she did not know what to do with him.

Obviously, the Park faced a costly, time-consuming, and self-perpetuating dilemma if every gorilla born to its collection had to be hand-raised. So, when Dolly became pregnant again in 1974, curator Jim Dolan was determined, if at all possible, not to end up with yet another human-oriented gorilla baby. He hired Steve Joines, then a graduate student in physical anthropology at San Diego State University, to train Dolly in the fundamentals of motherhood.

"My first problem was in overcoming Dolly's shyness," said Joines. "Gorillas either take to you quickly or not at all. Fortunately, we hit it off right away." Working in the back bedrooms, he began by showing her movies of gorillas in the wild in which the females were taking care of their own babies. But Dolly was much more interested in the projector and the two-dimensional images flashing on the wall than she was in what those images were doing. The motion pictures were not real and she knew it. Forced to rethink his strategy, Joines then came up with the idea of using a doll.

"We used a very simple pillow doll at first just to see her reaction. I told her the pillow doll was a baby and she trusted me that I wouldn't lie to her. From the beginning, she treated the doll differently from an ordinary toy. That's when we came up with a second, more realistic doll baby. Gorillas understand verbal commands fairly well, so I started with the command, 'Pick up the baby, Dolly.'"

Binti, shown here holding onto Dolly, was the first gorilla baby to be raised within a family unit at either the Park or the Zoo.

Dolly with her baby, Mary Ellen, who was born in 1981

Limiting his instruction to this for the first few days, Joines rewarded Dolly with a soybean or piece of apple whenever she responded to his directive correctly. Eventually, he succeeded in training her to respond to a series of commands to "Show me the baby" (so that sex and condition could be determined after delivery), and to "Be nice to the baby" (meaning to cuddle it); in this way, Dolly was slowly learning what to do with the baby once it was in her hands. When he realized that Dolly was just as likely to pick the doll up by its feet as its head, he taught her a new command, to "Turn the baby around." Although Dolly never confused Joines's words, her attention span was limited. After about twenty minutes, he could sense she was becoming impatient with the lessons for she would start to pat the doll a little too vigorously. So, they rested or played for thirty minutes before going back to work.

Dolly gave birth at night (on October 2, 1974), when nobody was around, but Joines remembers the moment when Dolly first showed him Binti as the proudest of his life. "The only crisis occurred later that day," he recalled, "when Binti began to cry and Dolly looked confused. After all, her doll baby had never cried. I told her to 'Be nice to the baby' and when she picked Binti up and began to cradle and comfort her, I wanted to celebrate." Within a week, Dolly no longer required prompting, and she nurtured Binti just as she had been instructed. For the first time, the Zoological Society of San Diego could boast a captive-born gorilla that had been raised completely within the troop.

Dolly had a stillborn male in 1978, and would not give birth again until June, 1981, but this time nature took its full and

Dolly holds Mary Ellen in one hand as she picks up some browse to eat with the other.

Trib, Dolly, and Mary Ellen out on exhibit

natural course, with no prior "coaching" proving necessary. Equally amazing, keeper Sue Kennedy was actually on hand for the early-morning birth of Mary Ellen. On all previous occasions, with the exception of the stillborn, Dolly had given birth at night and the babies had not been discovered until the next morning. This time, Kennedy was already at work, hosing down the sleeping quarters, when Dolly went into a sudden, quick labor in her bedroom. "I heard her vocalizing," Kennedy recalled, "so I looked around and saw her bobbing up and down, grunting, and patting herself. I shut off the water, watched her for a few seconds, then ran outside to telephone the vet. By the time I came back, she was reaching behind her as the baby slipped out. Then, she pulled the baby around and started cleaning her off. I was so excited I was in tears."

After a few minutes, Dolly brought the baby over to Kennedy who was standing at the bars. "She held the baby up and I said, 'Good girl, Dolly . . . Pretty baby, Dolly.' Since she seemed comfortable presenting the baby to me, I reached through and just lightly touched it. I wanted to try to establish contact with the baby as soon as possible, so that Dolly would trust me in case we had to handle the baby for any reason. Mostly, though, I just talked to her softly and tried to calm her down, because she was extremely nervous for hours after delivery. She was constantly cleaning the baby, cleaning herself, and trying to lick up the blood on the floor. There were acacia branches in her bedroom and she would make a little nest and sit in it, then get up and move the nest somewhere else and sit down. I talked to her a lot just to let her hear my voice and to reassure her that everything was all right. It was a hot summer day and I also kept giving her pieces of ice, which she liked to chew, and a lot of water from a cup. She had her own running water, but it's kind of a treat for the gorillas to drink out of a cup. This also meant that she was bringing the baby over, too, which enabled me to see if everything was going well."

Trib, a tender and protective father, accompanies Dolly and Mary Ellen during Mary Ellen's introduction to the main troop.

Mother and baby had been kept off exhibit for several weeks until Mary Ellen was old enough to cope with the other gorillas.

98

Mary Ellen looks up at her father, Trib, who holds some browse in his hand.

Within three weeks (as opposed to fifteen months with Jim and twenty-four months with Alberta), Dolly and Mary Ellen were released into the main exhibit to begin the introduction process: first with Trib, who was protective from the very beginning, and then with the rest of the family, including seven-year-old Binti, who immediately displayed an annoying, if understandable, case of sibling rivalry. "Mom had somebody else to watch after and everybody in the family was paying attention to this new baby," Kennedy pointed out, "so Binti responded by stealing the baby from Dolly at every opportunity, sometimes hightailing it to the other end of the exhibit with Dolly in pursuit. Trib would generally just sit and watch, until Mary Ellen screamed or Dolly was obviously agitated; then he'd go over and start grumbling and Binti would stop and cower in a corner until Dolly grabbed the baby back. Binti wanted to hold the baby just like her mother, and most of the time she would do it correctly, but she also treated Mary Ellen like a new toy, slinging her over her shoulder and running off, pounding on her, and just playing too rough. Finally, we just couldn't take any more chances, and we had to separate Binti from Dolly and Mary Ellen until the baby was old enough to fend for herself."

Meanwhile, Dolly had grown tired of being the patient, hovering mother that she had proven herself to be with Binti, whom she had carried around constantly for a full six months. An indication of this came when she was on exhibit with just Trib and Mary Ellen, for she would put the baby down next to Trib, and then go off to sit somewhere else. However, Trib enjoyed the baby's company and on a number of occasions he refused to let Dolly take her back, much to Dolly's annoyance.

Once Mary Ellen started crawling, Dolly found two-year-old Alberta to be a much more manageable baby-sitter (provided that Binti was not around to interfere). "Dolly would put the baby down and let her crawl away, then let Alberta go over and pick her up and bring her back," said Sue Kennedy. "There were also times when Dolly downright wanted Alberta to baby-sit. She'd either bring Alberta over and make her sit with Mary Ellen, or she'd take Mary Ellen over and sit her down next to Alberta, and then walk off to take a break from being a mother."

By the time Mary Ellen was a year old, Alberta's baby-sitting days were over, for the two had become willing playmates instead. Mary Ellen would go over to Alberta, climb up and

Binti harasses little Jitu during his introduction to the troop, just as she did with Mary Ellen a year earlier.

Jitu rides piggyback on Alberta, his older sister, who served as his protective baby-sitter out on exhibit. Alberta had provided the same care for Mary Ellen.

Keeper Sue Kennedy visits with Samantha, a gorilla brought in on breeding loan from the Erie Zoo in Pennsylvania.

wrap her little legs around Alberta's back, then go for a ride, just as she would on an adult. As little as Alberta was herself, she already knew how to carry a baby on her back, how to cuddle and be gentle with one, and how to hold one up to her chest properly. She had been able to observe Mary Ellen's grooming and nursing firsthand and had been allowed hands-on experience as well—just as she would have been in the wild. Binti, too, though overly aggressive with Mary Ellen, had still grown up completely within a family group and this experience would prove invaluable when, later, it came time for her to raise her own young.

Sue Kennedy had been working in the Park's Animal Care Center for nearly eight years, taking care of ailing, injured, and orphaned babies (of which Jim had been one), when she was named head gorilla keeper in 1979.

On a typical day, she comes to work at six-thirty in the morning, at which time the gorillas are usually sound asleep, lying on their backs or on their sides. She first gives them their morning meal—a spoonful of vitamin syrup followed by evaporated milk diluted with water—which they guzzle from a large, hand-held pop bottle. After finishing this meal one particular morning, Trib gave a low growl and then held his hand out for the daily allotment of eighteen prunes that he had been receiving ever since he had been placed on a constipating medication. "He prefers that I feed the prunes to him one at a time, like King Tut," said Kennedy, "but I don't have time to wait on him today." Still, Trib lay down to savor his prunes, placing them in his mouth one at a time, picking them clean with his teeth, then delicately taking the pits out with his enormous, but dexterous, fingers and dropping them to the floor. While Trib was thus engaged, Binti entered his bedroom, jumped up, and proceeded to pound her chest rapidly with her fists as though it was a kettledrum. "She's nervous because there's a stranger in here and she gets all worked up, but not because she's mad," Kennedy explained. "When Trib does it, we know he's upset about something. Now Alberta is doing it on exhibit, but she's just playing around, imitating the big guys." Whatever the reason, Binti went through her chest-pounding routine twice more before Kennedy went outside to clean the exhibit and hose down the moat.

By quarter-past eight at the latest, Kennedy lets the gorillas out on exhibit for the day, allowing them time to be alone before the Park officially opens at nine. Since Trib hates to sit on wet grass, he usually goes down to the wooden play structure early in the morning where, regal and supremely self-confident, he sits on high surveying his kingdom until the day warms up. Then he goes to a favorite spot right at the front of the exhibit where he likes to lie in the sunshine. "Trib is no longer much of an athlete," said Kennedy. "In fact, unless he's upset about something (which may provoke him to run back and forth across the exhibit), he's rather docile and laid back. But he does have a playful side. One day he pulled a loose pole off the play structure and it was like a new toy to him. He walked around with it in his mouth, all excited, and then he started chasing his son Jimmy, trying to hit him with the pole. Jimmy kept dodging the pole and they thought that was great fun."

Trib's basically gentle nature can also be seen in his relationship with Alberta, his "adopted" daughter. "She loves Trib and he just loves her," said Kennedy. "She'll go over and

Trib will sit there, put his arm around her waist, and hold her in his lap. Alberta looks back up at him and often reaches and touches him around the face." He also enjoys playing with Alberta—pushing her around, rolling her, and making her do somersaults. And whenever she is afraid of Binti, who loves to roughhouse, she runs to Trib and stands between his legs, as if to say, "Na, na, na, Binti—you can't get me now."

Alberta also enjoys entertaining the public as they stop to see the gorillas on exhibit. "She loves to show off," said Kennedy. "If the people clap their hands, she claps her hands. She somersaults and they all laugh, so she somersaults again, or does something else just to keep them going. When she was a baby in the Animal Care Center and the public could look in through a window, she would act oblivious to them, but as soon as they would leave she would go over and bang on the window, trying to get them to come back. Then she'd watch for new people to come by. That was her entertainment as a little kid, and she's still a little kid. But she's definitely a gorilla now. She has adapted very well."

The gorillas are brought back inside late in the day and given their main meal: monkey chow biscuits, which have all the necessary vitamins and minerals, the mixture of evaporated milk and water, fruit, and vegetables. Trib, who weighs about 480 pounds, has a closely monitored diet that includes three apples, three oranges, a couple of bananas, a couple of carrots, and an onion.

Unfairly portrayed over the years as ferocious, mindless jungle beasts, lowland gorillas are bright, sensitive primates who, when reared in captivity, often show affection for their keepers. Sue Kennedy, for one, certainly enjoys their company. "They're something else," she said. "On cold mornings, I used to go over to Jimmy's bedroom and say, 'Jimmy, can you warm up my hands?' I'd put them through the bars and he'd take them and pat them, or smack them, or just hold them to get them warm. He could have ripped them off if he wanted, but I trusted him. He was so gentle.

"One day, I came to work after getting my hair cut. My friends down at the Care Center didn't seem to notice the change and I thought, 'Well, nobody notices.' So, I came up here and I went through my usual routine, going down the line of bedrooms and checking on all the gorillas before I fixed their breakfast. As I came back, I noticed that Jimmy was flipping his head from side to side, so I walked over and said,

A planned matchmaking attempt between Trib and Samantha turned into a snarling fight. Samantha then had to be kept separate from the Park's troop until she could be moved to the Zoo in 1981.

'Well, what's the matter with you?' He put his hand through the bars, so I put my face up close and he touched my hair. Within a minute he had noticed that something was different about me."

Both gorilla species (lowland and mountain) have had their numbers so drastically reduced in the wild, the result of habitat destruction and poaching, that one observer has described them as "an international treasure on the edge of extinction." While naturalists and conservationists fight to save gorillas in Africa, concerned zoo administrators are doing the same on their respective home fronts, realizing as they do that every successful captive birth is a critical contribution to the world's overall gorilla population. Thus, Trib himself is a treasure, having sired five offspring—Jim, Binti, and Mary Ellen at the Wild Animal Park, and two youngsters born to females who honeymooned at the Park and gave birth elsewhere. At the end of 1982, a little over 400 lowland gorillas lived in zoos throughout the world, and of this number about 115 had been born in captivity.

While the Wild Animal Park, after years of painstaking effort, had finally developed a self-sustaining troop by 1981, the Zoo's breeding program—suffering from attrition, unsuccessful breeding loans, and the transfer of young males such as Trib to the Park—had reached a standstill. So, when Abe, an imported male from the Cheyenne Mountain Zoo in Colorado Springs, failed to mate with Bouba in 1981, curator Diane Brockman decided to start from scratch with new gorillas.

First, Abe was dispatched to a zoo in Texas and Bouba, the aging spinster who was one of Albert's original "sisters" at the Zoo back in 1949, was shipped to the Erie Zoo in Penn-

After Bouba rebuffed the natural advances of Abe, a Cheyenne Mountain Zoo male, and artificial-insemination attempts by Zoo researchers proved futile, she was sent to the Erie Zoo to share an exhibit with a sterile male gorilla.

Zoo officials hope for offspring from Alvila and Jim, both of whom were transferred from the Park in 1981.

Occasionally, gorillas will walk for several yards in an upright position, as Jitu does here.

sylvania to take up residence with a sterile male. "Bouba is a nice old gal," said keeper Ken Willingham, "and she's lived here for over thirty years, but you can't get too attached to your animals if you're serious about captive breeding. You've got to trade animals and move them around, like we're doing now, or you'll limit your breeding potential."

These moves at the Zoo cleared the way for three gorillas from the Park: Alvila, Albert's only offspring, who had produced two youngsters at the Roeding Park Zoo only to have her mate, Freddie, die; Samantha, who had arrived on breeding loan from the Erie Zoo in 1979; and Jim, Trib's firstborn, who would now get his chance to be a troop leader. (One reason Abe had been removed in the first place was because it was feared that he and Jim could not peacefully coexist.)

"Jim's a sweety and I'll miss him," said keeper Sue Kennedy before his move to San Diego, "but it's time for him to break away from his family and start a group of his own. He's lived here all his life and it's going to be a hard way for him to grow up, but we don't have any other choice."

Indeed, since gorillas form strong social attachments, Jim had a difficult time adjusting to the Zoo; instead of being his normal outgoing self, he was unhappy and withdrawn for weeks, and he lost weight because he refused to come in at night for his evening meal. Yet, finally, he began to accept his new home. Pretty soon, he was steadily gaining weight and, equally important, he started mating with both Samantha and Alvila.

This good news, however, was tempered by a tragedy at the Park, where Mary Ellen contracted an airborne virus (acanthamoeba) and died in less than a week. Fortunately, a two-year-old male, Jitu, was already in the process of being introduced to the troop, and Dolly transferred her maternal affection to him, thus hastening the transition for both of them.

Jitu, Alvila's second offspring, is Alberta's brother and had been hand-raised at the Roeding Park Zoo. "Actually, Jitu's strongest attachment has been to Alberta," Sue Kennedy noted. "She's more his size and he feels safe around her. When I come to work in the morning, they're still fast asleep, cuddled up together right next to Trib." Now that planning is underway for three additional exhibits adjacent to the present Gorilla Grotto, Jitu may well inherit his own troop there someday.

King Tut

OTHER FAMOUS AND IMPORTANT ANIMALS

n addition to the gorillas just mentioned, there are many other individual animals and groups of animals—past and present—who are deservedly important themselves, whether because of their personalities, uniqueness, special appeal to zoogoers, or significance for the future survival of their species. Here, then, is their story.

KING TUT, THE ZOO GREETER

Perched on a stand under a ficus tree across from the main entrance, King Tut, a Moluccan Islands cockatoo, is the venerable greeter for the Zoo's many visitors. He is also the resident of longest standing at the Zoo, having arrived in March, 1925, as a donation from Frank Buck, the "Bring 'Em Back Alive" animal dealer. When the weather is agreeable, King Tut spends his days entertaining the public out on his perch. He sleeps overnight in a warm back room inside the bird yard. "He's a grand old bird," said Art Risser, the general curator of birds. "In his prime he was a guest on many TV shows and it's rumored that he fan-danced with Sally Rand. He's showing signs of old age [a cataract in one eye and feathers

that don't come in properly] but he still puts on a neat show when he's in the mood. He sits on his perch, goes through his little dance with his head waving, and squawks at the people watching."

CHARLIE, THE ABYSSINIAN GROUND HORNBILL

The Wild Animal Park has the world's largest collection of captive hornbills. About twelve different species are maintained, most of them in off-exhibit cages where they can concentrate on breeding and nesting, sheltered from public scrutiny and commotion. However, just off the Kilimanjaro Hiking Trail, living in a large enclosure with his mate, is Charlie, an Abyssinian ground hornbill. Charlie is not only a remarkably successful breeder, but a colorful personality to boot.

Hatched in the wild in Africa, Charlie came to San Diego in 1951, as an adult, via the Rotterdam Zoo. Eventually, he was paired with a female from Holland and, though they failed to produce any offspring, Charlie seemed to enjoy life at the

Zoo. Although his wings were clipped, or pinioned, to keep him from flying away to Mexico, his cage had no top; so every morning he would jump out and walk around the grounds, visiting his favorite keepers and haunts. When he was ready to return to his pen, he would go to the bird yard, tap on the door of the office there with his beak, and have a keeper take him home.

In 1971, when Charlie's mate died, he was sent to the Wild Animal Park (before it had actually opened to the public). He was placed in the 110-acre East Africa exhibit, where construction was still going on, and was soon dubbed the Park's "sidewalk superintendent," as he poked his inquisitive beak into nearly every activity. "He's a very outgoing bird and he just wanted to be with people," said curator Carmi Penny. "He loved to get in a keeper's truck and ride next to the driver, just looking around out the window. Other times, he would trot alongside the truck and follow us wherever we went."

In 1972, Charlie was joined by Suzie, who had also lost her mate at the Zoo and who, like Charlie, had failed to produce any offspring. Undaunted, Charlie proceeded to court Suzie, winning her affection, and eventually they produced the first captive-raised ground hornbill outside of Africa. By 1982, they had produced another twenty-one babies and were still going strong, becoming the only pair of ground hornbills at the Park to reproduce with any regularity.

At first, Charlie and Suzie were allowed to nest out in the main East Africa exhibit, and Charlie would become extremely aggressive when Suzie was nesting. "He would let me go over to the nest and look at the eggs or the youngster," said Carmi Penny, "but he would absolutely terrorize most other people who got too close. One day, when Suzie was on the nest, two maintenance people had some work to do nearby. We warned them not to go in front of the nest, but they ignored us, and Charlie attacked. These two guys ended up on *top* of their truck, with Charlie pacing around down below, and they literally had to call for help by walkie-talkie to get out of there."

Charlie once took a hunk out of Penny's thigh while Penny, dressed in shorts, was bent down working in the exhibit ("He was just in a bad mood that day"), but otherwise they enjoyed a friendly relationship. "When Charlie was out in the main exhibit, we used to go hunting for food together. I'd take him down into a canyon where there was a lot of vegetation and I would dig with a shovel and Charlie would harvest all the

bugs and worms. This was a regular routine that he expected every day. When we moved him into the enclosure where he is today, we had a big population of mice. So, periodically, I'd go through with a hose and start filling up mouseholes with water, and Charlie would go to the exit holes where he would catch the mice as they tried to escape. He would pile them up, and then when he figured he had enough he would take them to Suzie and start feeding her. It didn't matter if she was nesting or not—this was her treat. He even taught a couple of his youngsters to do that."

The inquisitive Abyssinian
ground hornbill Charlie stands
watch as Park veterinarians and
keepers tend to a zebra.

BLACK JACK, THE UGANDA GIRAFFE

Majestic and dark-colored, Black Jack has sired all thirteen of the Uganda, or Baringo, giraffes born at the Wild Animal Park, and his offspring will soon be helping to create important new breeding groups at other zoos and reserves. He's not only a prime herd sire (the dominant male responsible for breeding), having impregnated eight of his female companions in 1982, but a favorite of Park personnel too. "The thing that impresses me about Black Jack," said curator Carmi Penny, "is that he's an extremely proud animal. Most of the other giraffes are chowhounds; they follow the food truck and will eat out of the back of the truck with no reservations whatsoever. But not Black Jack. For many years he was too dignified to stoop to the level of begging or stealing food from a truck—even special treats like carrots, apples, sweet potatoes, bananas, monkey chow biscuits, grain, lettuce, or cabbage. The competition from the other giraffes finally made him decide he had to take food out of the truck itself if he expected to get his share of the goodies. But he still won't let you touch him."

Black Jack was born at the Zoo in 1967, on the birthday of the famous World War I general John J. ("Black Jack") Pershing. He moved to the Park in 1971, and sired his first calf, Shangaza, in 1974. "The mother had trouble in labor," Penny recalled, "and we had to take the calf to the Animal Care Center overnight. The next day, we tried to reintroduce the calf to its mother, out in the main exhibit. This was before we had a boma [a sheltered corral] to keep the mother and calf isolated from the rest of the giraffe family, so we had to use a truck to keep Black Jack blocked off. Since giraffes are extremely curious animals and we didn't know what his initial reactions would be, we tried to play it safe. At first, we managed to keep him away by just moving the truck back and forth, staying between him and the mother and calf. But he soon had enough of that and he reared back on his hind legs and jumped completely *over* the truck. We hadn't anticipated something like that, but he didn't do any harm to the baby. He just wanted to investigate this strange new creature."

Until recent years, most zoos featured reticulated, or Somali, giraffes. However, the existing stock in captivity has become badly hybridized and now serious-minded curators are concentrating on the Ugandas, which are still purebred and in need of attention as their numbers decrease in the wild. Fortunately, they are breeding well in captivity.

Black Jack, on the left, neck-jousts with a younger male. This was a friendly encounter, but in the wild, two rival males will engage in this "necking" behavior during the breeding season, swinging their necks to deliver powerful blows to one another.

Closeup view of the Uganda giraffe's coat pattern. Body coloration usually darkens with age and is most dramatic in mature males.

113

THE MHORR GAZELLE

The Mhorr gazelle, one of the most beautifully colored and rarest of the antelope species alive today, typifies the cooperative efforts that are needed to try to save an animal from total extinction. Experts believe that the Mhorr gazelle is already extinct in its Sahara Desert habitat, and it is a known fact that fewer than a hundred animals are now in captivity worldwide.

Responding to the Mhorr's plight, and also to that of the severely threatened Cuvier gazelle, an intense rescue project—sponsored by the World Wildlife Fund—was established in 1971 on a private reserve near Almería, Spain. "The object," said general curator Jim Dolan, "was to breed these endangered antelope and then introduce the spin-off [excess offspring] back into their former range in North Africa. Well, in 1979, all these countries were approached, but none of them felt they had the money or the trained personnel to carry on a conservation project like this. So, the intermediate step was to spread the Mhorrs around to non-African collections. The director in Almería had more than seventy animals—perhaps the world's entire population—and he was starting to panic, worried that a disease might wipe them all out."

Subsequently, shipments were sent to Frankfurt, East Berlin, and San Diego. Three adult Mhorr gazelles were eventually put on exhibit in San Diego and, although shy and skittish by nature, they adjusted so well to their new Zoo environment that two females were born in February, 1982—the first Mhorr births ever recorded in the Western Hemisphere.

Although one baby had to be hand-raised by keepers in the Zoo's Small Animal Nursery (it died soon after), the other was properly cared for by its mother—yet another encouraging sign of adjustment to captivity. The next move: to establish a breeding group at the Wild Animal Park (with the Mhorr ideally joining the Cuvier gazelles and other desert-type animals in one large exhibit), and, from there, to work toward the day when offspring can finally be reintroduced back into North Africa.

These three Mhorr gazelles, who arrived at the Zoo in 1981, formed the first breeding group in the Western Hemisphere.

MASSA, THE LOWLAND GORILLA

Of all the gorillas to live at the Zoo and the Park over the years, few have been as mischievous, energetic, and athletic as Massa, a lowland gorilla who was captured in Gabon, Africa, in 1966. Raised at Dr. Albert Schweitzer's famous hospital in Lambaréné, Massa came to San Diego in 1968, as a gift from Schweitzer's daughter, Rhena. He lived at the Zoo until 1972 and was then transferred to the Wild Animal Park, where he quickly became a star performer in the large Gorilla Grotto that had recently been built there.

Steve Joines, who was to play such an important role in the Park's gorilla troop, wrote in ZOONOOZ: "As Massa grew older he developed into a remarkable athlete. During the hot summer months, he entertained visitors by making fantastic leaps from the grassy exhibit area into the water-filled moat of the enclosure. In addition, he quickly discovered that he was more than strong enough to dismantle the large, dead oak trees which were originally placed in the exhibit. Before Massa tore all of them down, one of the keeper's routine jobs was to haul oak branches out of the moat into which Massa had thrown them."

On other occasions, wrote Joines, Massa's athletic prowess caused his keepers some tense moments. "For example, there was the morning when eight-year-old Massa was more impatient than usual to leave his bedroom and get out into the main enclosure. The gorillas' retiring quarters [the off-exhibit bedrooms] are separated from the main enclosure by 500-pound galvanized steel doors that are operated by the keepers with a crank attached to a heavy steel cable. Normally it takes about thirty seconds to open one of the doors, but on this morning Massa was impatient; so when the door was lifted far enough for him to fit his hand under the bottom edge, he simply took the door with one hand and threw it straight up along its runners. The metal door rang like a bell, Massa scurried outdoors in the flash of an eye, and the hapless keeper was left with about eight feet of slack cable, cranking for all he was worth to prevent the door from slamming down like a 500-pound guillotine."

In 1978, after Massa and his intended mate, Alvila, had failed to produce any offspring, he was sent to the Los Angeles Zoo to live with their four resident females in a newly rede-

Athletic, water-loving Massa enjoys getting sprayed by a hose while out on exhibit at the Park.

signed gorilla enclosure. No sooner had he been released from quarantine than he was running around his new home and diving into the water-filled moat. A week later, he climbed a tree in the exhibit and discovered a group of younger gorillas living in the next enclosure. A 15-foot rock wall separated the two enclosures, and had hitherto been successful in containing the resident gorillas (including two adult males who had died before Massa's arrival), but Massa proceeded to catapult over the barrier with one mighty leap.

Since Massa was a bit too athletic for their needs, Los An-

geles Zoo officials returned him to the Wild Animal Park. Six months later, he contracted San Joaquin Valley fever, or coccidioidomycosis, a virulent infection of the respiratory tract that proved fatal. "Massa's passing marked the loss of a dear friend to the many employees who had worked closely with him, and to the thousands of visitors who had followed his development and enjoyed his antics over the years," noted Steve Joines. Fortunately, Massa's contemporary, Trib, is not only a proven breeder at the Park but an admirable troop leader as well.

KAKOWET, THE PYGMY CHIMPANZEE

Zoo keepers and visitors alike lost a special friend in 1980 when Kakowet, the rare and popular pygmy chimpanzee, died of heart failure. Not only did he leave a legacy of favorite stories, but also ten living offspring—nearly a third of the thirty-three pygmy chimps then living in captivity worldwide. (The pygmy chimp—about two-thirds the size of the common chimpanzee—is generally regarded as the closest primate to humans in terms of superior intelligence, personality, behavior, and even genetic characteristics.)

When Kakowet arrived in San Diego in 1960, from the zoo in what is now Kinshasa, Zaire, he was one-and-a-half years old and weighed only 15 pounds—a "peanut," or *cacahouète*, the French word from which his name derives. He was placed in the Children's Zoo, but as he grew older he learned how to jump out of the small ape exhibit, which he shared with the gorilla Trib, the orangutan Roberta, and the chimpanzee Lucy. On his first escape, he discovered the Natal plum trees growing beside the duck pond and he proceeded to gorge himself with plums. He broke out in giant hives—swellings the size of a quarter all over his body—which had to be reduced with antihistamines. Whenever he succeeded in jumping out of the exhibit, he would head for the plum trees and subsequently break out in hives; the problem was finally resolved when he was transferred to the main Zoo grotto.

In 1962, a six-year-old female chimp named Linda arrived, a gift from the Antwerp Zoo in Belgium. She and Kakowet were introduced and immediately became fast friends. At that time, they were the only pair of pygmy chimps in the United States and over the next eighteen years they contributed to the survival of their rare and threatened species by producing three males (Kevin, or K. C., Kalind, and Kakowet, Jr.) and seven females (Linette, Laura, Lorel, Leslie, Louise, Loretta, and Lana).

On and off exhibit, Kakowet and Linda formed a lively and affectionate group with their offspring. "Kakowet only weighed about 95 pounds," recalled keeper Gale Foland, "but he had a beautiful build, like a weight lifter; when he walked around you could see every little muscle in his body. He was also incredibly sensuous. If you got close to the bars when he was in his retiring quarters, he would reach out and softly caress your face with his fingers. Then, if you'd stroke him with your hands, he'd sit there and eat it up. He was always really gentle with Linda, too, and he loved to play with his kids. His favorite game was to have the kids in his lap as he tickled them. They'd be laughing—sort of a hoarse sound—and he'd shake his head from side to side with his mouth open, obviously enjoying himself."

Opposite:
Kakowet, the famous pygmy chimpanzee, runs across the front of his enclosure to greet someone he knows among the visitors.

Linda, Kakowet's longtime mate, holds one of their offspring. In 1981, after Kakowet's death, Linda was sent on breeding loan to the Yerkes Primate Research Center in Atlanta, Georgia, the only other facility in the Western Hemisphere to maintain pygmy chimps. She has since given birth, and has been joined there by two of her Zoo-born daughters, both of whom have also had babies.

BOB, THE BORNEAN ORANGUTAN

With his jocular jowls, his whimsical expression, and his sheer size (nearly 325 pounds), Bob was one of the Zoo's most photogenic animals. He was three years old when he arrived from the island of Borneo in 1958 and he lived another twenty-two years, leaving ten offspring behind him, all of whom are carrying on his line in zoos from Brazil to China.

"Bob was a really good animal," says keeper Gale Foland, "and I don't want to run him down, but he did have one unfortunate trait: he was somewhat of a wife-beater. The orangs are asleep when I come to work in the morning, and when I'd wake Bob up, he would proceed to roll his mate around the cage for about five minutes. He wouldn't bite Maggie, but he'd get down low and shoulder her about, roughing her up. Rather than fight back—which she knew was futile—she'd go into passive resistance and just take a little abuse. After that, Bob would be fine the rest of the day. I guess he was trying to impress me; it certainly wasn't for her benefit."

Veteran keeper Harold ("Mitch") Mitchell recalled one of Bob's more benign morning rituals. "In good weather, when we let him out on exhibit, he'd always climb to the top of the play structure for a look around. If the sun was out, he'd put a hand up to shade his eyes and lie there, watching the people as they watched him."

It is estimated that less than four thousand orangutans now survive in the tropical forests on the islands of Borneo and Sumatra. They are protected there, yet deforestation threatens their ultimate survival in the wild. Although there has been hybridization of Borneans and Sumatrans in captivity, the San Diego Zoo maintains a strong, separate genetic line for each. If purebred, the Borneans are easily distinguishable from the Sumatrans, for the former have characteristic cheek flanges and a heavier build.

After Bob died in 1980, the Zoo's Bornean colony fluctuated and curator Diane Brockman tried different ways of populating the group, searching for the right chemistry. She tried to incorporate Billy, a proven breeder from the Lincoln Park Zoo in Chicago, but he attacked the San Diego females—biting them severely—instead of mating with them. Then Brockman decided to let nature take its course with ten-year-old Ken-Alan, one of Bob and Maggie's offspring who was reaching sexual maturity. Sure enough, he mated with Mary Fred, a wild-born orang, and in March, 1982, she gave birth to Kent.

Opposite:
The Bornean orangutan Bob

Bob on the play-structure platform

Otis, the patriarch of the Sumatran orangutan colony

Karta, a Sumatran orangutan, hitches a ride on the neck of her mother, Jane, traveling as she would in the jungles of Sumatra. Born in 1982, Karta is the first orangutan to be mother-reared at the Zoo in many years.

OTIS AND THE SUMATRAN ORANGUTANS

Otis is Bob's younger counterpart in the Sumatran orangutan colony. A distinguished father (he had sired seven offspring by the end of 1982), he is also, in keeper Gale Foland's view, an even more impressive physical specimen than Bob. "Otis is just as big, but he doesn't carry around as much fat. We've been watching his diet."

"Otis is a pretty nice male," Foland noted one morning, as he stood next to the orang's bedroom cage, just before letting him out on exhibit. "When he's in a really good mood he sticks out his tongue so that I can scratch it, but right now he's upset about something and he'd bite me if he got the chance. He also likes to spit water at us once in a while."

Otis has an interesting lineage. His mother, Suma, was rescued as an orphan in Sumatra and brought to the San Diego Zoo by an American seaman in 1952. She was eventually sent to the Roeding Park Zoo, where Otis was born in 1965. He was transferred to San Diego the following year.

One of Otis's current mates is Bubbles, who has been on breeding loan from the Phoenix Zoo since 1977. Raised in that zoo's nursery, she took part in an animal act which consisted of sitting at a table and feeding herself with a spoon, then taking the dishes to a sink and turning on the faucet to rinse them. Even today, Bubbles will reach through the bars in her bedroom, take a spoonful from a bowl with food in it and feed herself. In Phoenix, she also learned to whistle by imitating the thick-billed parrots who lived in a nearby enclosure. Unfortunately, despite these talents, she failed to show any maternal concern for her first three babies (all sired by Otis) and they had to be hand-raised, just as she was before them. Jane, a wild-born orang on breeding loan from the Lincoln Park Zoo in Chicago, has had two babies since arriving in San Diego, and, unlike Bubbles, she has proven herself to be an excellent mother.

THE KOMODO "DRAGON" MONITOR

The Komodo monitor—commonly known as the Komodo "dragon" because of its size and its forked yellow tongue—is the largest living species of lizard, and a spectacular member of the Zoo's reptile collection. San Diego is the only zoo in the Western Hemisphere to have Komodos on display, and the species is extremely rare in the wild. Its native range is restricted to a small, remote group of islands in Indonesia, which government authorities are trying to protect from human encroachment.

In late 1980, San Diego had a male and two females in its collection, and Jim Bacon, the general curator of reptiles, felt they might produce offspring. There had been only one previously known group of captive-hatched Komodos, and the male in San Diego was the last survivor of that group of six hatchlings.

Alas, one of the females died, most likely from a liver infection. An autopsy revealed that she had completely non-functional ovaries. "She was fourteen years old and should have been in her prime," said Bacon, "but her ovaries were so tiny, they looked infantile."

Later, the other female was tested for hormone function, and when she failed the test the implication was that, for whatever reason, she, too, was neuter. "So, as far as we're aware, there's no hope for reproduction with this female, no matter how often the male makes his contribution," Bacon concluded.

Although the Komodos will continue to be a special project of the Reptile Department, all efforts so far to find a reproducing female have proved futile. One outside gamble was taken in late 1981, when Bacon had an ailing female flown over from the Basel Zoo in Switzerland. She was a proven egg-layer, but she died soon after her arrival, the victim of a blocked and diseased colon which, surgeons found, was distended by seven pounds of rodent hair, bones, and eggshells. San Diego and three other zoos (in New York, Philadelphia, and Miami) have since formed a consortium in hopes of acquiring a large group of wild-born Komodos through the Indonesian government.

The Komodo "dragon" monitor is the world's largest living lizard; the male in San Diego's collection is nearly ten feet long. Endowed with formidable claws and sharp, serrated teeth, male Komodos in the wild have been known to bring down 1,000-pound water buffalo.

This male Komodo was acquired from the Basel Zoo in Switzerland in 1976. His relatives are seldom seen in zoological collections and are protected by the Indonesian government.

THE GALAPAGOS TORTOISE

One of the most important conservation projects in Jim Bacon's Reptile Department involves the continuing effort to help propagate the Galápagos tortoise in captivity. Lumbering about their large, grassy exhibit on Reptile Mesa, the thirty-odd Galápagos tortoises—some of them hatched at the Zoo as long ago as 1961—constitute the second-largest colony in captivity, not including that which exists on the Galápagos Islands, their native habitat. Yet, the San Diego colony has had virtually zero population growth in recent years, posing serious questions about this species' future survival—at least in captivity.

When Jim Bacon came to the Zoo in 1975, he instituted a number of changes in tortoise management, hoping to raise the fertility rate among the eggs laid. In years prior, although eight hundred eggs had been laid, only thirty-six of them had contained hatchlings. "So," said Bacon, "we changed their diet from a predominance of lettuce to more of a variety of green leafed foods; we started feeding vitamin and mineral supplements to each tortoise; we added proper nesting soil, banana tree trunks, and different browse [Zoo-grown plants which supplement the diet]; and we made some changes in the social structure, removing several pugnacious individuals. Then we crossed our fingers. Lo and behold, they laid a lot of eggs and we had thirteen successful hatchlings in 1976. But to be honest, we didn't really know if it was just luck, or a result of the six or seven changes we made, or a combination of two or three changes. We didn't know what the key was, but we thought we had found it, so we stayed with the changes."

Unfortunately, though eggs were laid over the next five years, not one turned out to be fertile. Then, in 1981, only one egg was laid, and this by a female known only as "No. 4"—a female who had been laying infertile eggs practically every year since 1959. "Obviously, we didn't have much hope with that egg," said Bacon. "But we incubated it in the Reptile House and 134 days later it became the fiftieth tortoise to hatch at the Zoo." Tom T. Tortoise, as he was named (though "he" could very well turn out to be a "she"—the sex of a tortoise cannot be determined for several years), weighed only about two ounces and measured only about two inches upon hatching, yet one day he could grow to weigh 500 pounds.

The Hood Island tortoise has a distinct shell, the front edge of which is much higher than that which appears in other subspecies. The shell's additional height enables this tortoise to stretch its long neck high enough to reach the top parts of cactus, its primary food source in the wild.

This Galápagos tortoise at the Zoo represents one of the eleven subspecies still surviving in the Galápagos Islands.

LASAI, THE INDIAN RHINOCEROS

"Lasai is the ultimate as far as Indian rhinos go," said Carmi Penny. "It's like having a family pet that weighs 8,000 pounds and is worth $100,000." Penny knows, of course, that Lasai is actually priceless in terms of helping to preserve his severely endangered species (which is the largest of the rhino species), for he is a proven breeder in captivity and a mellow animal to work with—in most instances.

"From my standpoint," said Penny, "the Indian rhinos symbolize what our role is all about at the Wild Animal Park. We give them living space and a lot of special attention because of their status in the wild and the difficulty in maintaining them in captivity." Victimized by human encroachment and poaching, only an estimated eleven hundred rhinos survive in the Asian wilds today, and they have nowhere left to go except to protected game reserves. Barely a hundred Indian rhinos are now in captivity in the world's zoos, and less than ten have been born in the Western Hemisphere—three of them to La-

Lasai, the Indian rhino, cools off in the stream that runs through his Asian Plains exhibit. Indian rhinos have a single, short horn, not nearly so lethal a weapon as that which appears on the southern white species. As in all rhinos, the horn is composed of keratin (a fibrous protein) and is not firmly attached to the skull. It grows throughout a rhino's lifetime and will grow back if broken off.

Gainda, born in 1978, looks like a miniature warrior clad in a coat of armor as she trails behind her mother, Jaipuri. Indian rhinos appear virtually indestructible, with their covering of thick skin and characteristic wrinkles or folds, but even scratches will draw blood.

sai. In addition, only the Wild Animal Park and the Los Angeles Zoo currently have viable breeding groups in this part of the world.

Building an Indian rhino breeding program at the Park has been a long, demanding, and oftentimes frustrating, struggle. The project began in 1971 when Lasai was sent to the Park from the Zoo, where he had been living unsuccessfully with Jaipuri. "There wasn't enough space and they didn't get along," Penny explained. "He kept beating up on her and they never did breed." (Lasai had been born in the Basel Zoo

in Switzerland in 1962 and hand-raised in its highly successful Indian rhino collection.)

After Lasai had adjusted to his new home in the Asian Plains exhibit at the Park, Jaipuri was brought in and this time all went well between them. (She had been wild-bred in India, but raised in a game reserve.) They had two offspring, but both died soon after birth—a costly loss of reproductive years, considering that the Indian rhino's gestation period is sixteen months.

Trying to increase the reproductive odds with Lasai, the Park imported Golden Girl, a rhino that had been loaned to them by the Philadelphia Zoo in 1977. This proved an ill-fated introduction. "We know now that as long as a female acts submissive, either by running away or being sexually receptive, Lasai is not going to be dangerous," said Penny. "But the first time he approached Golden Girl, she responded aggressively, swinging her horn at him, and he just couldn't handle that behavorial response. He took off after her, hitting her severely with his horn several times and finally running her off a hillside into some big rocks." Battered and gored, Golden Girl died four months later from internal injuries.

Finally, there was a breakthrough in captive propagation when Gainda was born to Jaipuri in March, 1978. She survived successfully, yet not without a scare at about four months of age when she had a severe bout of diarrhea and stopped nursing. Since baby rhinos normally gain 100 to 120 pounds a month for the first year, getting Gainda to eat was critical. She wouldn't take any solid foods because she hadn't been weaned yet, but when then veterinarian Lester Nelson tried to give her peanut butter—which was similar in texture to the medicine she was being given—she liked the taste and began licking it up. Pretty soon, the vets were able to add other supplements to her daily jar or two of peanut butter, and then she was able to start nursing again.

"We don't think of rhinos getting mutual satisfaction through grooming, or being tender with each other, so it was fascinating to see the interaction between Gainda and Lasai," said Carmi Penny. "We had Jaipuri and Gainda locked up in a small maternity boma inside the main exhibit [for safety purposes], but we built 'windows' into the structure so that Lasai and the baby could make contact, if they wanted. Lasai would stick his head through one of these windows for thirty minutes at a time and let Gainda lick him, and then he would position himself in different ways so that she could cover new areas."

Thus, father and daughter already had a strong bond when it came time to separate Gainda from Jaipuri, five days before Jaipuri gave birth to Pandu in August, 1980. Gainda was distressed by the separation—which was necessary for her own safety—and for weeks would cry for her mother outside the boma, but, fortunately, she had Lasai. "Gainda was left all by herself, without mom, but here was this big lovable hunk of rhino, Lasai, who accepted her," said keeper Rick Barongi. "We were extremely fortunate to have a male with such a good disposition. A year later she had become a pest with Lasai; he had taken over the mother role and she wanted to be by him all the time, but he's a normal male rhino and he just wanted to sleep and be by himself all day. He didn't like having to socialize with Gainda [or with Jaipuri and Pandu once they had been released from the boma], yet he tolerated her. She always slept next to him and if she got too close or touched him, he'd snort and throw his head around, but she knew he was all bluff, that he wasn't going to fight. When he allowed her to be around, she would groom him constantly, just licking him all over his body. She loved it and he liked it—but he didn't like it all the time."

One day, a television crew from San Diego came out to the Park to do a feature on keepers Barongi and Rick Cliffe. Barongi suggested a segment involving Lasai, "to show viewers that size doesn't have to be related to danger." They assured the interviewer, Jeannie Miller, that Lasai was a mellow rhino and that it was really not dangerous to get close to him.

"Okay, that's great," said Miller. "I'll stand in front of Lasai and you guys feed him carrots while you tell me what you like best about being a keeper."

"When we got out there," Barongi recalled, "Rick and I were nervous about the interview and we forgot to notice, as we set up, that Lasai was cornered. He had the moat wall behind him and our trucks were to his left and right. Suddenly, as we were talking, he snorted and swung his head up, which is a warning he's getting ready to move. I said, 'Here, take another carrot,' but it was too late. He was excited and he took off, straight ahead. Jeannie Miller was already running away, but in the only direction Lasai could go. He ran toward her at first, but then purposely sidestepped her and ran off. He didn't want to hurt her, he just wanted to get out of there."

As a result of this episode, those who work around Lasai know that, as tame as he normally behaves, he is still a rhino, with millions of years of survival instincts bred into him.

The Indian rhinos will remain a top-priority project at the Wild Animal Park in the coming years, even though the effort to secure their future seems slow and uphill at times. A second exhibit—solely for Indian rhinos—is already being built and will house a new breeding male from India (purchased for $49,000). Even a third exhibit is being planned, which might have Pandu as its herd sire. "I'd certainly like to see at least ten females here, and maybe three bulls," said general curator Jim Dolan. "Reproductively, this is not a species that is dropping calves every nine months. The female has a long gestation period, and then the calf is nursing into the second year; so a female is only producing one calf about every three years. Knowing how endangered they are in the wild, we must make sure we're shored up with captive adult animals at all times, so that we can perpetuate our breeding program."

THE KOALAS

The most famous residents at the Zoo have long been the koalas, a marsupial (and not a bear) that is native to Australia. San Diego received its first koalas in 1925 (both of whom died within two years) and over the years other small shipments followed. In 1976, however, as a Bicentennial gift from the Australian government, the Zoo received six Queensland koalas—all previous shipments had been comprised of the more hardy New South Wales koalas—and serious husbandry efforts with this particular subspecies began. Bolstered by a 1981 shipment, the Queensland colony is now thriving and proving that koalas have a lot more personality than is commonly thought.

Of that Bicentennial group, only two males, Cough Drop and Waltzing, and one female, Matilda, survived the first year in San Diego. One of the females who died, however, had a baby in her pouch and this koala was able to survive through hand-raising.

"Gum Drop was about seven months old," said Jane Jacobson, the keeper in charge of koalas, "and he had only been out of his mother's pouch about a month. But fortunately he was already eating eucalyptus leaves [a koala's sole diet], so we didn't have to worry about fixing a formula." Still, since he needed round-the-clock attention, Zoo veterinarian Jane Meier offered to become his surrogate mother until he was old enough to fend for himself among the other koalas.

At Meier's house, Gum Drop was given a barrel-like home to live in, a contraption with several compartments covered with carpet which served admirably as a substitute pouch.

Gum Drop, who arrived from Australia in his mother's pouch in 1976, was orphaned when about seven months old. He was then hand-raised for six months by Jane Meier, a Zoo veterinarian, who housed him in a compartment covered with carpet and eucalyptus branches.

Feeding was a bit more difficult. At first, Meier would either cut fresh eucalyptus browse or bring it home from work, then sit there, practically sticking each leaf in Gum Drop's mouth. Eventually, he learned to sort through browse and feed himself and also to drink water from a cup, though koalas normally get all the moisture they need from their eucalyptus diet. One of his favorite pastimes was to ride around on Buck, a gentle border collie, clinging to Buck's thick coat just as though the dog was his mother.

Gum Drop would also go to work with Meier. When he was about a year old, she started bringing him into the Koala House and leaving him for an hour or two every afternoon so that he could grow accustomed to his future home—and to the other koalas. Eventually, he was staying all day, then all night; and soon he moved in on a permanent basis. He was given a separate cubicle and a special little tree with small branches that were easy for him to grab. Then he had to learn how to sleep in his perch tree like a regular koala. "Since he hadn't grown up in a tree with mom, acquiring that special sense of balance koalas have, he had trouble maintaining his balance when he slept," said Jane Jacobson. "He fell out of the tree several times [without getting hurt] until he learned how to secure himself in the branches." Since koalas like to sleep or doze in the fork of a tree for eighteen to twenty hours each day, this was a rather important breakthrough.

Easing Gum Drop's transition into the group was the protective and nurturing Carol, a New South Wales koala (who has since died) who was descended from a group that had arrived in 1960. (The Zoo's current koala clan consists entirely of the Queensland subspecies.) "Carol showed extremely maternal instincts toward Gum Drop," said Jacobson, "and actually became like his aunt. Every afternoon we'd let him wander around in the hallways so he could explore and climb up onto the ledges and begin to feel comfortable about the place. Whenever he got himself into a situation where he didn't really know what was going on, he'd give his juvenile distress call, and Carol would come down from her tree and go looking for him. If she couldn't find him, she would come to me or to Jane Meier and put her front legs up on us as if to say, 'Where is he? Do you have him?' She would be upset until she found him."

Gum Drop and his "aunt" spent a lot of time together, making his introduction to the other koalas that much easier.

One day, for example, Cough Drop—a somewhat crotchety older male—was harassing Gum Drop in one of the trees. "Carol went over and got between them," Jacobson recalled, "and then she faced Cough Drop and had a screaming fit. He just backed off, right down the tree, because he wasn't about to fight with her if she was that mad."

Raising Gum Drop demanded long hours of patience and effort, but it paid off, for he grew up to be a normal koala—not a "people" koala—and his son, Pooya, was born in December, 1980, to Matilda.

Matilda, the only surviving female from the Bicentennial shipment, had given birth to three other koalas before Pooya, but only Koobor (born in February, 1978) had survived. Obviously, more females were needed to boost the colony's population. "I felt like I was basically taking care of a museum exhibit, as far as reproductive success was concerned," Jacobson admitted. Then came the crucial breakthrough in 1981, when the Zoo obtained six females and one male from the Lone Pine Koala Sanctuary in Australia. Within a year, one new baby had emerged from its mother's pouch and three more were on the way.

Jane Jacobson now had a population explosion on her hands, and a diverse group of koala personalities to contend with. There was Euc, for example, a juvenile male who had arrived in 1981. Though he was only two years old, he was already the largest resident in the Koala House. "I have never seen a personality quite like his in a koala," said Jacobson. "He's very aggressive and he has an independent spirit." He also proved right away that he was an escape artist, not about to stay confined in his 15-by-20 foot cubicle at night. "Most of the koalas are content to just stay put," Jacobson noted, "but Euc seemed to have a strong territorial instinct, possibly because he was wild-born [he was later orphaned and then hand-raised in Australia]. Whenever he escaped, we usually found him in a different place inside the barn; so, apparently, this was his territory and he was simply staking it out and learning where everybody was." After about a dozen escapes, the keepers decided to extend a plastic cover over the top of Euc's cubicle walls (which are about five feet high) and to shorten his perching tree (to about four feet) so that he wouldn't be able to climb up the tree and jump out. "He wasn't doing

Koala in the fork of his perching tree

any harm at first, but we were afraid he might come into contact with one of the older males—Cough Drop or Walt [Waltzing]—and get hurt in a fight. Also, as he grew more sexually mature, we didn't want him visiting the females without our knowledge. We want to keep our breeding under control by knowing who the parents are."

At one point, Jacobson said of Euc, "He's handleable if you are firm and you tell him, 'Okay, Euc, I'm going to move you, so stop swinging at me—and don't bite!'" Yet, as he grew into a young adult with long, sharp claws, he became far less accommodating and increasingly dangerous to handle. The koalas must be handled so often—to take them out on exhibit, to move them into other cubicles for mating, to weigh them periodically—that Jacobson had to begin a daily regimen aimed at modifying Euc's biting and clawing behavior. If he tried to bite, she would say "No!" and if he did not stop, an assistant would blow a whistle. If Euc persisted, she would spray him in the face with water. "Within a couple of weeks, we noticed definite improvements," said Jacobson. "We also began introducing him to more of the females as they came into estrus, and this helped calm him down."

The six females who arrived with Euc were a decidedly mixed bag in terms of personality. On the one hand, there was Peg—"Just the typical timid soul, who seems to be constantly in fear that someone is going to do something awful to her," said Jacobson. "When I put Cough Drop out with her and two other young females to see if we could get some breeding going, Peg spent the entire ninety minutes sitting at the top of one of the trees and wailing for dear life whenever Cough Drop came near, as if to say, 'Please don't hurt me, I'm only a child.' Needless to say, she wasn't ready to become a mother." However, when she came into estrus six months later—bellowing loudly which is a good sign that a koala is in heat—she was placed in Gum Drop's cubicle and was receptive to his advances.

At the opposite end of the spectrum was Jan—"a real Miss Piggy," said Jacobson. "She's a very aggressive female who will squawk or bite or even fight to get what she wants, whether it's some fresh browse that has just been put up, or a desired perch position. The highest fork in a tree is a favored spot, so usually she or Matilda will be up there." She, too, mellowed somewhat after having her first baby in 1982 (this was Cough Drop's final offspring).

When the 1981 koalas arrived, Matilda's forced adjustment provided interesting insights into koala behavior. "Until they arrived," Jacobson noted, "Matilda had always had a 'room' of her own and her own tree, so she never had to compete for food or a perch position. As a result, she was pretty much of a blob, without much personality. Then, one day, we needed her cubicle as an isolation area for Katja, who was pregnant. This meant that Matilda had to start sharing a group of three trees with five other females and her one-year-old son Pooya. She proceeded to spend the first two days sitting in the highest part of one tree, screaming and just having a fit if anyone so much as came near her: 'Get out of my tree—this is *my* tree!' After a while, however, she adjusted to the situation quite well and learned to move around peacefully within the group. She's still somewhat of a queen bee, and the pickiest eater of all the koalas (she has to have the best of the browse or she won't eat it) but, overall, I think putting her with all the others was the best thing we could have done for her."

In working with the koalas day to day, Jacobson is firm when necessary, but generally accepting of their individual quirks. "Walt will do anything for you if you just scratch his back first, but scratching instantly puts Cough Drop in a bad mood." She also caters to their eating whims because she wants a healthy, contented colony. "Animals are not going to breed if they're not happy and feeling comfortable in their environment. So, it's very rewarding knowing that I'm helping the koalas feel that they're in a natural enough situation for breeding to take place."

Considering the relatively small number of koalas in the San Diego colony, genetic management is critical if as large a genetic pool as possible is to be maintained. When a female comes into estrus, she is isolated with an adult male who has been selected after careful consideration of several factors. "We want to keep as many male bloodlines going as possible," said Jacobson, "and we want to prevent one male's bloodline from becoming too predominant. We also 'encourage' certain pairings, such as the one between Euc and Katja, both of them wild-born."

If mating takes place, no other males are placed with the bred female. Even if she comes into estrus again the following month, the same male is used so that there's no question as to who the father is if and when she becomes pregnant.

The koala's gestation period is just thirty-five days. At the end of this period, a single baby is born, usually measuring about three-fourths of an inch—or roughly the size of a peanut. Though the baby is not fully formed at birth, it has fairly well-developed forearms and tiny claws, which it uses to climb from the birth canal opening up into the mother's pouch. Here it attaches to a nipple, spending the next three to four months just eating and sleeping, by which time a person can start to see some movement in the pouch and a fairly evident bulge. Not until about six months of age does the baby begin to peek outside.

"Once breeding takes place," said Jacobson, "we must wait and let nature take its course before we know for sure that the mother has a baby in her pouch. An exact birthdate is hard

Koala reaching for a branch. "You have to be careful when you're handling koalas," said keeper Jane Jacobson. "They are cuddly, but they also have long sharp claws."

to establish because the newborn is so small, and if we're not around when the birth happens—especially at night—then there's generally no evidence left several hours later. One thing you absolutely never do is peek. Down in Australia, they found that when they were opening up the pouch and looking inside, they had an extremely high incidence of death in pouch young, resulting mainly from infection and contamination. Since it isn't necessary to do that, we're content to wait a couple of months."

Once the baby crawls outside of the mother's pouch, the next six months are critical in terms of mortality. Jacobson doesn't even count newborn babies as actual members of the colony until they are about eight months old. "Until then, you just never know," she said. "Arthur (Matilda's third-born) showed every indication of being a big, strong, healthy baby when he came out of the pouch, but just overnight—for some unknown reason—he died."

A group of koalas, partially hidden by freshly cut eucalyptus browse, peer out from their tree perches in the Koala House.

As juveniles and adults, koalas require as much careful daily observation as any other group of animals at the Zoo. "Koalas can be deathly ill and show no signs of it," said Jacobson, "so it's important that we pick up on very subtle signs that something might be wrong, like runny eyes or an uncharacteristic behavior. One day, I noticed one of the males breathing really hard out in the sunroom, so I brought him into the shade but he kept breathing hard. That was enough to pick up on, so I called the vets and they came down and started him on antibiotics right away. He came back strong, but there's no telling how sick he might have become if we hadn't caught it in time.

"Another thing we've learned that is critical to koala health is the amount of stress they incur. Most of the koalas go outside on exhibit where the public can see them, but not Matilda. Until we decided to just keep her inside all day, she would sit out there hanging on to the tree for dear life, her eyes bugging out. We knew that that kind of experience certainly couldn't be good for her health."

Since changes in health are not always indicated by variations in eating habits and other behavior, each koala is weighed at least two to three times a week and the results are plotted on a wall graph to make trends more obvious. Once, when Jacobson noticed that Cough Drop's weight was declining, the veterinarians examined him and found two loose teeth that had apparently been curbing his interest in eating. The teeth were pulled and in two weeks his weight began to increase.

Prior to 1976, the koala exhibit was basically an open grove of tall trees surrounded by a low protective wall. The koalas were mostly kept in one large group, with no organized breeding program and no isolation areas for pregnant females or mothers with pouch young.

All this changed once the Bicentennial group arrived. In order to provide an ideal breeding environment, the off-exhibit bedroom area was built, incorporating the successful husbandry concepts developed at the Lone Pine Koala Sanctuary in Australia. This building provides shelter and a climate-controlled environment; sunlight streams through skylights and forced-air heaters are used when necessary. Canvas curtains take the place of windows and can be opened throughout the building to allow for fresh-air circulation in good weather. Movable interior partitions make it possible to rearrange sleeping areas and to create maternity and reproduction cubicles when these are required. The females are able to live in a communal setting, but the older males—with the exception of Gum Drop and Pooya, who get along fine as father and son—must live alone to prevent some rather fearsome fighting.

Adjacent to the building is an outside enclosure with several trees, where, weather permitting, the koalas are brought out for public viewing. As tree-loving animals that are certainly not inclined to climb down and run around the exhibit, the koalas can usually be seen munching on eucalyptus leaves or dozing in the foliage. A new elevated walkway now allows visitors to observe koala "activity" *inside* the building as well. "Koalas sleep so much that people always ask me, 'Do they make any noise?' " said Jacobson. "Well, the males can bring the roof down when they're vocalizing and the females give out a rather terrifying shriek."

San Diego is one of the only locales outside of Australia able to sustain a koala colony, thanks to an abundance of eucalyptus trees in the local area. At one point, since koalas subsist entirely upon eucalyptus leaves, stems, and the tender tips of branches (as well as on the seedpods and flowers at certain times of year), Ernie Chew, the Zoo's former horticulturist, decided to conduct a two-year "taste test" to determine which species of eucalyptus they preferred. The koalas were allowed to feed on two hundred species, of which eighteen proved more palatable than the rest.

"We've actually found about twenty to twenty-five species that they like and will eat on a regular basis," said Jacobson. "These trees are grown on the Zoo grounds, while a fresh-cut supply is also sent from the Wild Animal Park five days a week. So we get a good variety—which is important, because koalas are very finicky eaters—and we know the trees haven't been sprayed with anything that might be toxic. We feed them from two to four kinds of browse a day, and we rotate from day to day so they don't get bored with the same kind of browse. We've found they have better appetites this way. Also, we basically let them dictate what they want to eat. This means we feed a lot of 'sucker' browse—tender young branches that come up from the base of the tree—as opposed to drier treetop browse. Sucker browse is richer tasting, with a higher moisture content, and they seem to thrive on it."

A great mystery about koalas is how they are able to survive, let alone thrive, solely on a eucalyptus diet. The leaves are rich in oils, alcohol, and cyanic acid—a combination that, by all rights, should have a detrimental effect on them. Yet, their digestive systems are somehow able to assimilate this food and they are able to get their total nutritional needs from it. "Unless they're ill," said Jacobson, "we don't bother with any type of mineral or vitamin supplements." Of course, the koalas' total reliance on eucalyptus presents a scary problem. "If they're not willing to eat the fresh eucalyptus you're giving them, you're in deep trouble. There's no way you can force-feed them [this has been tried and has not been successful in the past] or give them anything as a substitute that will sustain them."

Jacobson gives her colony anywhere from 100 to 125 pounds of browse a day—"more than they can possibly eat"—for this ensures that if any of the browse is wilted or tainted they will still have plenty of good browse to choose from. She marvels at the way they pick through a particular branch, stripping one stalk clean but sometimes leaving an adjoining stalk untouched. "We're still trying to figure out why they eat what they eat. For instance, when browse wilts, the cyanic acid levels build up in the tips of the leaves. But the koalas seem to know, without even biting off the leaf, if it is good to eat or not."

When it appeared that the koala colony could grow to nearly twenty individuals by early 1983, Zoo officials began talking about either expanding the present facility, or, as a more remote possibility, starting a second colony at the Wild Animal Park. Some type of action is obviously necessary, since the young males are proving to be sexually mature by the age of only two—and are in the company of equally receptive females.

ANIMAL ACQUISITION

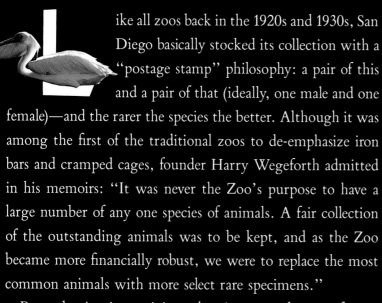

ike all zoos back in the 1920s and 1930s, San Diego basically stocked its collection with a "postage stamp" philosophy: a pair of this and a pair of that (ideally, one male and one female)—and the rarer the species the better. Although it was among the first of the traditional zoos to de-emphasize iron bars and cramped cages, founder Harry Wegeforth admitted in his memoirs: "It was never the Zoo's purpose to have a large number of any one species of animals. A fair collection of the outstanding animals was to be kept, and as the Zoo became more financially robust, we were to replace the most common animals with more select rare specimens."

Reproduction in captivity, when it occurred, was a fortuitous event—increasing the Zoo's population while providing an animal that could later be used in trade—but not a goal in itself. Nobody was much concerned about developing sustained captive-breeding groups then, nor worried about a possible future shortage of animals coming from the wild. There was no need to be, not when Wegeforth and other zoo directors could periodically leave on collecting expeditions to Asia and Africa and return home with hundreds of fresh new specimens to bolster their collections.

Of course, those years of abundant and available wildlife have long since passed, forcing all responsible zoos to alter drastically the methods they use when trying to create collections that are entertaining, reproductively viable, and at the same time conservation-oriented. No longer able to depend upon the wild as a continuing source of new animals for exhibit and off-exhibit breeding groups, zoos everywhere must rely heavily upon themselves—both individually and collectively. This new approach is expressed by Larry Killmar, curator at the Wild Animal Park: "Actually, it's no longer very practical for us to be going to Africa or Asia to secure animals. We'll always be working on shipments from there, of course, but it's an expensive, time-consuming process and there are many regulations that prohibit importation of certain animals because of disease factors. Besides, very few animals even become available. So, we're looking to *ourselves* as the wild, where the pressure is on to produce as many animals as we can—especially those that are listed as endangered. We want to meet our own needs on a continuing basis, while supplying zoos here and abroad."

An ambitious goal of the Zoological Society of San Diego

Chinese dholes, a type of wild dog, came to San Diego in 1979 as part of the first animal exchange with China.

Hoping to rely principally on reproduction within the overall collection, the Zoo would supplement the genetic stock when necessary through breeding loans, exchanges, and purchases from other zoos, wildlife reserves, and foreign sources. A growing self-sufficiency is certainly evident at the Wild Animal Park, where the mammal population has grown from 553 specimens (comprised of 73 species and subspecies) at the end of 1973 to 1,437 specimens (comprised of 116 species and subspecies) by the end of 1981. "Reproduction accounted for about 80 percent of that growth," said Killmar. "Whenever we add a new species, the initial breeding group includes only about two to six animals, because we rarely can find larger groups to bring in."

At all major zoos today, breeding loans and animal trades have become the most feasible method of sustaining a collection, both economically and logistically. Money helps, especially when an animal comes on the open market as an outright sale, but zoo directors cannot really buy their way to a serious collection. For one thing, endangered animals are seldom sold; for another, they are prohibitively expensive when they are (the Metro Toronto Zoo recently paid $120,000 for a pair of Indian rhinos). "Trade is the major way to go," said Carmi Penny, the San Diego Zoo's curator of mammals. "When it comes to animals already in the zoo world [as opposed to those imported from the wild], we can't simply sell our excess animals and buy the ones we need. In fact, most places are not interested in receiving money for their animals. They want to trade, because they need to keep their exhibits

Also included in the first Chinese shipment was a pair of Styan's pandas, the diminutive relatives of the giant panda.

filled and they want specific animals for their own breeding groups. So, trading animals or setting up a breeding loan is often the only way we can acquire new animals or unload our excess."

Trading exotic animals, Penny explained, is a bit like trading baseball players. "Basically, negotiations depend on what the market reflects: how common the animal is that you want to secure or trade away, how difficult it is to acquire that animal out of the wild, and how popular it is among curators and the public. Giraffes, for example, were relatively cheap in the late 1970s, but today they're extremely expensive, if you were to put a monetary value on them."

The fruitful, ongoing exchanges with zoos in China, which began in 1979, are all based on trade. In the first exchange,

for instance, San Diego acquired two rare species of Chinese mammals—Chinese dholes and Styan's pandas—and handsome groups of Derbyan parakeets and Jankowski's swans. In return, China received American flamingos and two adult southern white rhinos (part of the now-famous 1971 shipment from South Africa). The two rhinos weighed in at 22,800 pounds in Pan Am's airfreight depot, and the shipping bill came to almost $20,000.

"In negotiating with the Chinese zoo directors, it's obviously difficult to determine the relative worth of our respective animals, since some of them are common in one country but priceless in the other," said Clayton Swanson, San Diego's deputy director for collection management. "For example, when the goral [a goatlike antelope] were coming to

This tiger subspecies is commonly referred to as the Siberian tiger, but the Chinese call it the North China tiger. To prevent confusion, the international studbook keeper in East Germany has recommended that the name Amur be used as a compromise. A pair of these tigers was sent to San Diego by the Chinese in 1982.

us from China, I wanted to insure the entire group for $20,000. The shipper looked at me and said, 'You do mean $20,000 *apiece*, don't you?' I told him no, and he reminded me that they were priceless. I agreed—nobody else had them outside of China—but I just couldn't justify putting that much money into them." (Subsequently, the goral had to remain in East Germany, victims of hoof-and-mouth disease that was de-

tected while they were in quarantine there. However, San Diego still hopes to receive future offspring from these animals.)

The Chinese connection is important not only to San Diego, which has gained a number of new species for visitors to enjoy, but to the zoo industry in general. "We're bringing in new blood for species that already exist in this country but are badly

The brown eared pheasant, native to the forested mountains of western China, is considered an endangered species.

The Mandarin duck, cloaked in feathers of arresting color and ornamental arrangement, looks as if it is made of porcelain instead of feathers. In its native Japan and China, this bird is famous in art and literature as a symbol of marital fidelity.

The stunningly beautiful golden pheasant is a common bird in China. The male's gilt collar is fanned to veil his face during courtship.

The Himalayan Impeyan pheasant is one of the most beautiful of all game birds.

The Bulwer's wattled pheasant, which is distinguished by the vivid blue, well-developed wattle in adult males, is a striking inhabitant of Bornean rain forests. Five of these birds were donated to the Zoo by private aviculturists in 1980, and a number of chicks have since hatched.

inbred," said Swanson, "so collections should improve everywhere. About a half dozen different pheasants have arrived, along with three young Siberian tigers [which the Chinese call North China tigers]. The tigers in this country have been so inbred, they're relatively easy to obtain here, but new blood like this is extremely difficult to find—and very expensive, if you're shopping on the open market."

With wilderness environments, and hence wildlife, continuing to deteriorate at a frightening rate, zoos are cooperating as friendly rivals to an unprecedented degree. Having North America's only captive breeding group of a particular species may add to a zoo's overall public image, but the curators involved know that there must be a second breeding group, and a third, and a fourth before they can begin to breathe a little easier. Only by trading their excess animals, swapping unrelated animals, and arranging breeding loans can zoos minimize inbreeding problems and build the total captive population of a species to the point where it can withstand future setbacks.

The philosophy behind breeding loans is twofold. First, when San Diego sends excess animals to another zoo, the long-range goal is to help that zoo start or expand its own breeding group. Ideally, this in turn will produce less-related offspring that the Zoo can then draw upon should the need arise. Second, should San Diego lose its only breeding male or female in a certain species—or even lose an entire group due to catastrophic illness—a curator can recall the animal or animals on loan and provide a new mate or start a new group.

In order to keep their options open, San Diego curators try to plan each of their breeding groups years in advance. When Mark Rich was in charge of the polar bears, he talked about his youngest cub, Nanuck. "I'll have to move him out eventually, because I don't want him to breed his mother. He'll be the first polar bear that I don't sell or trade, since I want to establish a breeding loan and help make sure we can eventually get an unrelated animal back here. Nanuck's father, our breeding male, will probably last another fifteen years, but in case something happens to him I need to have a backup somewhere else. I could either trade Nanuck for another male, or if Nanuck is in a zoo where he's breeding and has a male offspring, I could trade that young male for an unrelated male to come here as our breeder. Should our only reproductive female die first, however, I might have to use Nanuck as trad-

Black swans courting at the Park. Dutch explorers were amazed when they first saw black swans on a river in Western Australia because until that time all swans were believed to be white.

The California brown pelican, once so severely endangered that it was headed toward extinction, has made an encouraging comeback since the federal government banned the use of DDT in 1972.

The fire-tufted barbet, indigenous to the high mountain forests of Malaya and Sumatra, is a colorful resident of the Zoo's Tropical Rain Forest Aviary.

Victoria crowned pigeons, noted for their beautiful lacy crests, were first brought to the Zoo from New Guinea in 1923.

One of the most beautiful of all owls is the snowy owl. Although it lives in Arctic tundra regions, it has been known to winter as far south as Texas.

ing material. So, it's complicated, but that's the situation we all face."

Even when the Zoo has animals out on breeding loan, the loss of an adult mate can still mean years of searching and waiting until an unrelated new mate can be found. This is especially true for species like the siamangs and gibbons, that are rare in captivity and in which the adults form monogamous pair bonds.

Such was the case for Sam, a siamang who was in his prime when he lost his mate in 1976. Since no other zoo could be found with a spare female—and a mateless siamang male is better off by himself until a male with a mellow disposition can be found as a cagemate—Sam had to live alone for five years. Finally, Nancy was obtained from the zoo in Jakarta, in exchange for a pair of ring-tailed lemurs. "Just accomplishing that took two years of paperwork, trying to get all our permits to mesh," said curator Diane Brockman. "So, it was a major event when we were finally able to introduce her to Sam. Yet, even after all our efforts, we had no assurance that the introduction would work. When a male siamang lives alone for such a long period of time, he can develop neurotic behaviors that will often continue when he's put with a female."

Thus, Zoo keepers knew they could not simply put Nancy in Sam's cage and hope for the best. They first placed her in a small cage on wheels and rolled it up next to Sam's bedroom, behind his exhibit cage, so the two could see each other without being able to reach through the bars and cause any harm. "They took to each other instantly," Brockman recalled. "Both of them got as close to their bars as they could and they started hooting, which is territorial communication. Later on, they started chattering back and forth—a friendly, low-keyed type of communication. Over the next couple of days, Sam spent a lot of time in his bedroom visiting with Nancy and it seemed obvious there would be no problem, so we decided to put them together. Within ten minutes there was copulation and we stopped worrying."

The next morning, Sam and Nancy were lounging around their enclosure, alternately snoozing and grooming each other,

The geographic range of the Old World white pelican is a vast one, extending from Europe to Africa.

Nearly thirty polar bears have been born at the Zoo since 1932, including Nanuck, shown here with his mother, Bonnie.

A grizzly bear performs for pass-
ersby.

a telltale sign of closeness and cohesive behavior among nearly all primates. "Look at them," said Brockman. "Aren't they tender? They're like honeymooners."

"This was a real headache," she added, "just to get one animal safely here, but it was worth it. And I'm sure Sam agrees."

One of the most encouraging and important advances in terms of zoo cooperation came in 1972 with the formation of the International Species Inventory System (ISIS), which some people have referred to as a computer dating service for exotic animals. Funded by over 120 member zoos and based independently at the Minnesota Zoo, ISIS was established to help avoid a Noah's Ark approach to zoology—with two animals at this zoo and two animals at that zoo, and no exchanging or meaningful reproduction going on. Since then, the American Association of Zoological Parks and Aquariums (AAZPA) has targeted several dozen endangered species for special attention in regard to captive breeding, and the pedigree and breeding records for each of the captive animals within those species have been sent to and stored in an ISIS computer. The ISIS director monitors this information and then recommends specific breeding loans or exchanges that will best utilize a particular species' genetic pool. If, for example, he discovers that a zoo has two breeding-age males but only one is being used because the other is too closely related to the breeding female, he will alert the AAZPA's conservation coordinator. This person will in turn talk to the curator of the zoo in question, "suggesting" where his unused male should be sent, so that it, too, can begin producing offspring. (Zoo curators can also initiate contact with ISIS and learn where to find a genetically suitable mate for a particular animal.)

An excellent testimony to inter-zoo cooperation can be found in the International Okapi Breeding Project—a project which also serves to illustrate the kind of juggling and maneuvering that is necessary when trying to build a prized species' numbers in captivity.

Shy and elusive, the uniquely colored okapi was unknown to science until 1901, when Sir Harry Johnston discovered what he thought was a new species of forest zebra in the jungles of the Congo (now Zaire). Actually, as naturalists soon learned, the okapi's closest living relative is the giraffe, with whom it shares such similarities as the shape of the head, the long neck,

San Diego's siamangs call to one another from their island exhibits every morning, using their inflatable throat sacs and vocal cords to produce loud, distinctive hoots that can be heard throughout the Zoo.

and the foot-long prehensile tongue which it uses when stripping tree branches of their leaves—its main food source in the wild.

The okapi is extremely rare in captivity, with less than sixty now living in zoos around the world, including those at the San Diego Zoo and the Wild Animal Park. San Diego's first okapis arrived from Africa in 1956, and, eventually, one of the calves from that group, Mokolo, was transferred to the Wild Animal Park to begin a breeding herd. He was joined by Kamina, a female on loan from the Cheyenne Mountain Zoo, and their first offspring was born in July, 1980. Neglected by his inexperienced mother, Afmadu had to be raised in the Park's Okapi Care Unit. But when Kamina gave birth to Bambesa in October, 1981, she took proper care of the baby from the beginning. Nevertheless, keepers posted a twenty-four-hour watch on mother and baby for several days since okapi babies are susceptible to many diseases and thus have a high mortality rate. (A second female, on breeding loan from the Brookfield Zoo in Chicago, was later introduced to the pair so she could observe natural maternal behavior.)

"Okapis are worth in excess of $100,000, so it speaks well for the Cheyenne Mountain Zoo that they loaned us their only female okapi [in exchange for an unrelated okapi from another zoo]," said general curator Jim Dolan. "It was also a far-sighted thing for the people at Brookfield to say, 'Okay, we're sitting here with an animal that's incredibly valuable, but for the continuation of the species—at least in North America—it's vital that we move her out of our collection.' Chicago's only male was this female's father and they wanted to avoid inbreeding, so they called a symposium of all the zoos with okapi and we agreed to start shipping animals around to make the best use of the available blood stock."

This decision set off a chain reaction: the Chicago female was sent to the Wild Animal Park to mate with an unrelated bull; Oklahoma City and Dallas swapped bulls (giving Dallas a bull that had originally been imported from the Frankfurt Zoo); and exchanges were arranged with European zoos which were also faced with the problem of inbreeding. A woman in Antwerp now runs a world studbook for all okapi in captivity and she decides, based upon bloodlines, where their offspring should be placed.

Dolan expressed the sense of urgency shared by all those concerned about the okapi's future. "Every birth in captivity is incredibly important to the survival of okapis," he noted. "Since we don't know how many exist in the wild—and nobody is having much luck getting them out—captive-breeding programs may be the only chance of survival for this species. Also, most of the okapi in captivity today are aging animals and we have to get reproducing groups going before we lose the older breeders."

Although it's a rapidly diminishing option, San Diego curators still try to purchase animals straight out of the wild by working through reputable dealers. A wild-caught group of animals is always desirable, since it provides the Zoo and the Wild Animal Park with either a founding colony that can build on a strong genetic base, or individual animals who can introduce fresh new bloodlines to an already existing collection, thus reducing the potential ill effects of inbreeding.

Insights into the philosophy and process involved in bringing about such a difficult undertaking are provided by Diane Brockman's year-long effort to start the country's first viable colony of red howler monkeys from a group originating in Bolivia.

After receiving a master's degree from San Diego State University, where she wrote her thesis on the douc langur, Brockman was hired by the Zoo in 1976. She has since become the first woman curator in the Society's history. "When I started formulating a primate master plan, I intended to make an intensive effort with South American primates," Brockman explained. "That aspect of our collection had always been weak, and these primates need our attention now, while they're still available—before the rain forests are gone and before the governments there start closing the door on animal exports."

The red howler purchase was initiated by a dealer in Miami (the main port of entry for South American wildlife), who called Brockman and asked her if she would be interested in any red or black howlers. "I told him yes," she recalled, "but that first I needed to do some checking around. I contacted Dennis Meritt, Jr. [at Chicago's Lincoln Park Zoo], who is one of the most experienced people working with South American primates, and I asked him which of the howlers deserved the most work in terms of captive reproduction. 'The reds, without a doubt,' he said. 'They are much less resilient

Afmadu, a male okapi, stays close to his mother, Kamina, in their grassy enclosure at the Park.

Overleaf:
Like all newly arrived animals, this group of red howler monkeys from Bolivia had to pass through a thirty-day quarantine at the Zoo hospital before going out on exhibit.

to the stresses of captivity and they are rarer.' He also knew the dealer and recommended him."

Deciding to gamble on the red howlers, Brockman called the dealer and told him she wanted, ideally, three males and twelve females. She then put in a request for money, and the Zoo found a donor to foot the eventual bill of about $16,000.

Four months later, the dealer had finally put together a large enough group from his Bolivian suppliers and he called Brockman. "They're in, they look good, and I'll ship them," he said. Thirteen, instead of fifteen, actually arrived in San Diego (there were four males and nine females), but Brockman feared that some would be lost while in thirty-day quarantine. "These are such delicate creatures, especially when they are coming out of the wild and having to adjust to a captive diet, that I thought to myself, 'Okay, if only three die, we're in good shape.' We lost four, but the others adjusted well, and within a few months we had at least two pregnant females."

Once the howlers had settled into their corner enclosure in the monkey yard, Brockman managed to purchase another five females with which to start a second breeding group in an enclosure nearby. The arrival of this shipment seemed to be an especially fortunate development for Tom, the largest male in the existing group, for he had recently been supplanted by

Above:
The long-eared, or spectacled, elephant shrew is exhibited in only a handful of zoological collections, and was first acquired by the Zoo in 1978 when two pairs arrived from the National Zoo in Washington, D.C.

Left:
The Mindanao tarsier, distinguished by its round head and owl-like saucer eyes, is a relative of the lemur and is found only on certain Philippine and Indonesian islands.

Opposite:
The Canadian lynx, a secretive, nocturnal animal, lives in coniferous forests in Alaska, Canada, and northern portions of the lower forty-eight states.

Above:
Native to North Africa, the winsome fennec fox is the world's tiniest fox—standing about eight inches at the shoulder and weighing about three pounds—but possesses remarkably large ears.

Opposite:
The Asian lion is severely endangered in the wild—only about two hundred survive in India, all in the Gir Forest—and is far rarer in captivity than its African counterpart, with less than one hundred living in zoos worldwide. The Park has thus launched an ambitious Asian lion breeding program; two prides have already been established, stocked with nearly twenty lions acquired from six other zoos.

Jerry, the second-largest male, and actually driven out of the troop. "Tom and a female were attacked by the others and bitten rather severely, so we had to move them to the Zoo hospital," said Brockman. "When they recovered, we felt we had to try to reintroduce them to the group, but again they were attacked. We rescued them, but the female eventually died and we had to rig up a separate back bedroom for Tom until his harem arrived. I'd go by and visit him every day, and I tried to assure him that he would not always be living life as a solitary male." Alas, the new shipment of females turned out to be the wrong subspecies, and as Brockman is determined to maintain pure genetic lines, yet another order had to go out.

The obvious question raised here is: Why take the howlers out of the wild in the first place and subject them to such stress, especially considering the time and expense involved? "Many South American primates, like the howlers, titi monkeys, sakis, and others, will not be endangered for several years," Brockman acknowledged. "But species like these will inevitably become endangered. Most South American rain forests could be gone by the year 2000 and we probably won't see primates in the wild, so now is the time to develop our husbandry techniques, while we can still get them from there. We need to stay a jump ahead by building numerous breeding groups now, so that these various species can be thriving in captivity before the real crunch comes." She pointed out, as an example, that once a species is added to the Appendix One list of endangered animals ("virtually all primates will be on this list one day"), heavy restrictions and months of paperwork are added to the acquisition effort, thus making it far more difficult for a zoo to add the particular species to its collection.

All of the San Diego curators are actively working on ways to secure animals from the wild, whether through private dealers, foreign zoos, or government-run wildlife sanctuaries. But they enter into each negotiation knowing that once a deal is consummated, the process that follows will be fraught with seemingly endless paperwork, fights with nit-picking bureaucracies both here and abroad, and the sheer logistical problems inherent in shipping exotic animals and keeping them alive in transit. Curators joke that the correspondence involved in securing one single animal often weighs more than the animal

Above:
A baby Goodfellow's tree kangaroo pokes its head out of its mother's pouch while out on exhibit. The mother came to San Diego in 1977 as part of a shipment from Papua New Guinea.

Opposite:
This Count Raggi's bird of paradise, whose brilliant plumage and long tail feathers are typical of the male in this species, also arrived from Papua New Guinea in 1977. A pair of these imported birds produced a hatchling in 1981 which was the first chick ever raised in captivity in the Western Hemisphere.

Overleaf:
Grand eclectus parrots are noisy and conspicuous in the New Guinea rain forests. Extreme sexual dimorphism once led to the belief that males (predominantly green) and females (red with blue) belonged to different species.

itself. Every animal shipped from abroad must have a certificate of origin to prove that it has been legally caught and a certificate of health to prove that it has no communicable diseases. Then, export and import permits are required by the Convention on International Trade in Endangered Species—and these must mesh with the scheduled travel permits. If the animal is not transported before the permits expire, then the whole process must begin again.

"This process of acquisition is becoming more complex and expensive every year, and we have to fight our way through ridiculous fine points that are something to behold," said Art Risser, the general curator of birds. He knows from firsthand experience that once a shipment takes off, bound for San Diego, the real tension is only just beginning. "There are all these extenuating circumstances that we have no control over, like missed connections or extremely high temperatures during a long airport layover. All we can do is sit here and wait, knowing that any delays will add stress on the animals being shipped and increase the chances they won't survive."

One particularly hair-raising incident involved a shipment of tree kangaroos and five species of rare and colorful birds that were sent from Papua New Guinea in 1977. The shipment brought important new additions to the Zoo—notably a group of birds of paradise—but only after overcoming one bureaucratic snag after another.

After numerous delays in coordinating export and import permits, the shipment finally left a wildlife sanctuary in Papua New Guinea, but in order to travel by airfreight, the animals first had to endure a strenuous journey by road to Mount Hagen, and then by air to Port Moresby. This was followed by a flight to Manila and then Honolulu, with the ultimate destination being Los Angeles. All was fine in Hawaii until U.S. Department of Agriculture (USDA) officials discovered that the shipment's original quarantine destination was Los Angeles, and that, in the case of the birds, the prescribed routing had thus been violated by the landing in Honolulu. (These quarantine restrictions did not apply to the tree kangaroos, who were allowed to travel on to San Diego without delay). Federal law further prohibited the shipping of the birds from Honolulu to Los Angeles, so two alternatives existed: either the shipment could be destroyed or it could be re-exported to Manila, where it would then travel on to Los Angeles by way of Tokyo.

Only after strenuous negotiations (conducted in part by attorneys from the Zoological Action Committee—an organization established to help solve bureaucratic problems that arise with respect to zoos and government regulations) did the USDA allow at least the birds of paradise—an endangered species—to go through quarantine in Honolulu. The remaining birds, including Pesquet's parrots, Goldie's lorikeets, eclectus parrots, and boobook owls had to be rerouted through Manila. Remarkably, none of the birds in this shipment died, but three birds of paradise were lost in quarantine as a result of cumulative stress.

"I know that all of the government regulations are designed to discourage smuggling and ultimately protect wildlife,"

Tahitian blue lories have been described by one of their keepers as "dapper little birds in blue-and-white tuxedos." This pair of lories preen themselves while on exhibit at the Zoo.

Risser said later, "but it gets highly frustrating when there's really no logical reason for certain actions and the inflexibility of officials is putting precious wildlife through unwarranted stress."

Of course, as Risser acknowledges, the San Diego Zoo has also benefited from government efforts to curtail smuggling of exotic birds into the country. Confiscated birds are sometimes turned over to the Zoo without fanfare, but it took a celebrated incident involving the rare Tahitian lory to establish a favorable precedent.

Tahitian lories, which are found only on a couple of islands near Tahiti, are beautiful minute parrots, slightly smaller than

Purple-capped lory

the better-known lovebirds, but far more valuable and endangered. By the mid-1970s, with none having been seen in captivity since World War II, they had become one of the most highly prized birds in the smuggling trade.

Then, in October, 1977, private aviculturists in the San Diego area were contacted by two men offering to sell these birds for $7,000 a pair. Customs agents were notified and the smugglers were apprehended five days later, eventually pleading guilty to the crime. But what to do with the ten confiscated lories? By rights, since the smuggled birds had not met with quarantine requirements, they could have been destroyed by the USDA. This was a routine custom then, the purpose of which was to protect the domestic poultry industry and large avicultural collections from the threat of imported diseases. But customs officials in charge of the confiscated birds sought an exemption from this destruction rule. "Why not quarantine them to see if they're healthy and allow them to live?" they argued with impeccable logic.

So the birds were sent into strict quarantine at the Wild Animal Park until a decision about their fate could be reached. General curator Jim Dolan argued that the lories were "so rare that there is a real threat that they will be extinct in a few years," and he pressed the USDA to allow the birds to remain at the Park. Meanwhile, bird lovers everywhere rose up in defense of the lories, and the media, too, joined in, carrying the story of the birds' plight. Eventually, and partially in response to public opinion, the U.S. Attorney General's office issued a court order demanding that the birds be kept alive for use as evidence in the smuggling case. After that, the government decided that the smuggled birds could be quarantined for ninety days at the home of Rosemary Low, a noted lory expert, and then returned to the San Diego Zoo. Unfortunately, Mrs. Low lived in England, and she refused to ship the birds back again once the quarantine period had ended, arguing that it would put them through too much stress. So there they remained, with several pairs having since reproduced.

Still, the whole episode established an important precedent: that of exempting rare and endangered birds from automatic destruction after confiscation. This soon saved a second group of lories that was confiscated in early 1978. Although the birds had to be flown to Honolulu to be quarantined at the government station there, they were nevertheless returned to the San Diego Zoo. Finally, on May 3, 1978, all eight lories were

released into a remodeled aviary that included a small waterfall and lush landscaping that was reminiscent of their tropical habitat. The lories responded to this environment and the group eventually grew to as many as twenty-five birds before a sudden illness struck half of them down in 1981. New breeding pairs had to be formed, but reproduction resumed.

While most animals come to San Diego only after long months of careful planning and intricate negotiations, the overall collection does sometimes benefit from unexpected donations and fluke acquisitions.

Art Risser, for example, remembers the time when a man called from Texas, saying he wanted to donate a Papuan hornbill. "Since we have a keen interest in hornbills, we jumped at the chance," Risser noted. "When Beaker arrived, we didn't think he looked like a Papuan, so we checked his identity in a hornbill monograph and we discovered we actually had a Buton hornbill, which is an even rarer subspecies. In fact, Dr. Jean Delacour, a foremost aviculturist, told us this was the first one he had ever seen in person." After a three-year search, which involved working through the Indonesian ambassador to the United States, Risser was able to secure a female mate from the zoo in Jakarta.

Although Diane Brockman gets innumerable offers from people wanting to donate monkeys and other primates, she almost always turns them down. "The problem is, they've all been pets and thus oriented toward humans, so if we were to try to incorporate them into a social group at the Zoo, it wouldn't work; they would be abused by the group." She relented, however, when a couple in New York offered a pair

When a long-sought mate finally arrived for Beaker, the Buton hornbill pictured here, the new bird would not respond to his overtures and even attacked him on several occasions. The two were separated and then gradually reintroduced. As a precaution, several of the female's flight feathers were clipped, which slowed her down enough to allow Beaker to escape when necessary. They are now living together on exhibit.

The forbidding, toothy American alligator has staged a revival in the nine southern states where it is now protected by strictly enforced federal and state legislation.

The eyelash viper, whose native habitat extends from southern Mexico to Ecuador, has a prehensile tail well suited for life in a forest.

Black-tailed rattlesnake, coiled in its familiar striking position

Because the black-necked spitting cobra can shoot venom as far as ten feet through the air and thus temporarily blind an intended victim, the keepers never open its cage without first putting on goggles.

The green tree python's coloration is well adapted to its native home high in the tropical rain forests of New Guinea. The Zoo's python, purchased from the Steinhart Aquarium in San Francisco, is about five feet long and spends most of the day coiled and draped over a limb.

The Fijian banded iguana is a rare lizard—only about twenty are now in captivity worldwide—found solely on the Fiji and Tonga islands. The Zoo's original collection was a gift from Prince (now King) Tungi of Tonga in 1965, but the first hatchling did not arrive until 1981.

The green iguana, displayed at the Park, is a large tropical lizard found in Central and South America.

The Zoo's bearded dragon collection was enhanced in 1982 by the purchase of three such lizards from the Melbourne Zoo in Australia. When the lizard feels threatened, its beard, formed by a large fold of spiny skin across the throat, becomes erect. At the same time, it gapes its jaws, exposing its yellow mouth lining. Both of these defense mechanisms make the lizard look larger and more ferocious to would-be predators.

The range of the shovel-headed tree frog extends from central Mexico southward to Guatemala.

Brilliantly marked poison arrow frogs secrete a virulent poison through the glands in their skin. These secretions are used by many South American Indians as a paralyzing agent on the tips of their hunting darts.

of cotton-top tamarins. "This was a rare opportunity to get an endangered species," she explained. "Tamarins are also monogamous and do not live in social groups, so we wouldn't have an introduction problem. Nor had they been coddled." Once Brockman determined that they had been acquired legally and carried the proper papers, she moved them into an enclosure in the monkey yard. "They're beautiful young animals, they're adjusting very well, and they should be breeding soon."

One of the largest unexpected collections to arrive at the Zoo came into the Reptile Department's possession in 1981, when a local resident died after having been bitten on the hand by a venomous Indian cobra—one of thirteen poisonous creatures he had been keeping in his home. "He had about ninety snakes and other reptiles in his collection," said general curator Jim Bacon, "including monitor lizards seven or eight feet long, boa constrictors, eyelash vipers, a small alligator, and several rare rattlesnake species. The collection was diverse, valuable, and well cared for. Unfortunately, he got careless." The man's heirs were allowed to keep the common, garden-variety reptiles, while the poisonous and endangered species were released to the Zoo. In turn, Bacon donated the cobras to the Gladys Porter Zoo in Brownsville, where the curator had established a successful breeding program.

Then there are those animals who come to the Zoo as gifts from foreign governments, such as the pair of Manchurian cranes which Japan sent to San Diego in 1981. Typical of the way curators must operate today, Art Risser quickly integrated the cranes into his existing breeding colony rather than simply maintaining them as a beautiful spectator attraction. He paired the two Japanese birds with two cranes from China, thus insuring completely unrelated offspring. Then, he sent a female to the National Zoo's complex at Front Royal in Virginia to join their male, who was on breeding loan from the International Crane Foundation. In return, San Diego received a female from the foundation to pair with its remaining male.

So, with three pairs of these handsome birds, which are treasured in Japan as symbols of eternal youth and happiness, Risser looked forward to the challenge of working with an endangered species that is dependent on captive breeding. "These are rare and wonderful birds," he noted. "They will entertain Zoo visitors with their elaborate dances, and I hope they will cooperate in a breeding program through which we can provide offspring to other American zoos."

Of the Zoo's six Manchurian cranes, four were gifts from foreign governments. Zoological officials in the People's Republic of China sent one pair, and in 1981, the mayor of Osaka, Japan, sent another.

EXHIBITING THE ANIMALS

 grew up on a farm near Union City, Tennessee, in Mississippi River bottomland, and there were few neighborhood children around to play with," Carmi Penny recalled as he relaxed in his curator's office at the San Diego Zoo. "I had my sisters, but you know how that is, so I spent a lot of time by myself in the woods, hiking and learning about wildlife. Ever since I can remember, I always wanted to work with animals, and that's what I pursued."

In 1966, Penny's family moved to San Diego and he started college there the following year, eventually doing graduate work in biology. After landing a job at the Zoo in 1970 as a primate keeper, he was then transferred to the Wild Animal Park, where he had been hired as a keeper well before the Park's official opening. "Working there had been my main objective," said Penny, and he eventually became a curatorial field supervisor under Jim Dolan, an equally avid animal enthusiast who, unlike Penny, had grown up with plenty of neighborhood pals—on the sidewalks of the Bronx in New York.

Much as Penny enjoyed working at the Wild Animal Park, he moved back to the Zoo in late 1981 to become its curator of mammals (excluding primates). This was one of several key appointments that the Society made as it consolidated management of its overall animal collections, placing them under the direction of three general curators: Jim Dolan, mammals; Art Risser, birds; and Jim Bacon, reptiles.

Working with Dolan, Penny began to formulate a series of far-reaching plans to improve the way in which many of the animals at the Zoo were displayed. Drawing on ten years' worth of experience at the Wild Animal Park, and soliciting suggestions from Zoo keepers, veterinarians, architects, and landscapers, Penny and Dolan proposed that virtually every mammal exhibit be remodeled. At the time, a $2.5 million renovation of Bird and Primate Mesa (now called the Heart of the Zoo) was nearing completion—providing lively new homes for the orangutans, siamangs, pygmy chimps, and douc langurs while nearly doubling the size of the Tropical Rain Forest Aviary—and they wanted to keep this momentum going. Penny felt that exhibit improvements would give zoogoers a more educational and aesthetically pleasing experience. He also argued that upgraded exhibits would be necessary if the Mammal Department hoped to respond effectively to the increasing demands for successful breeding programs in urban

The aerial tramway, the Skyfari, carries Zoo visitors between the Reptile Plaza and Horn and Hoof Mesa, offering panoramic views of the Zoo grounds and the city of San Diego.

Completed in 1982, the first phase of the Heart of the Zoo renovation features multilevel wooden walkways which pass by the island exhibits for siamangs and the new enclosures for orangutans and pygmy chimps.

Sam and Nancy, two of the Zoo's siamangs, hang from poles in their new Heart of the Zoo exhibit while communicating with siamangs in an adjacent island enclosure.

zoos. The Wild Animal Park's success had certainly not lessened the Zoo's important efforts to achieve reproduction among its own mammals. If anything, since Dolan wanted to use the Zoo's status as a permanent mammal quarantine station to better advantage, by bringing in founding groups of endangered hoofed stock and then sending their offspring to the Park, its role had been enhanced.

"If we're willing and able to spend the money, there's a world of good we can do here," Penny said one day as he walked the Zoo grounds, describing the changes he would like to make. "We only have about 100 acres to work with, but there's actually a tremendous amount of unused space in these canyons, if we can just tear down certain exhibits and start over, while redesigning others."

Penny is primarily concerned with finding ways to enrich the living environment of the mammals on exhibit, for, as Zoo behaviorist Dr. Don Lindburg explains, "the overall quality of the individual exhibits affects the health and well-being of the animals, and thus their inclination to breed and reproduce." One way of fostering this sense of well-being is to replicate the animal's natural habitat wherever possible.

"Cement enclosures are easier to keep clean and in good condition," Penny acknowledged, "but outdoors, in the winter, a cement floor can get awfully cold and damp. Besides, in a tactile sense, cement can't be very comfortable for an animal accustomed to living on dirt or grass [or even for those born in captivity]. So, we're going to take a jackhammer to the cement in some of the exhibits, then fill them with dirt and

Three Speke's sitatunga in Cascade Canyon. These aquatic antelope are shy by nature and difficult to spot in the wild.

A pastoral scene at the Zoo's Cascade Canyon

plant trees and other vegetation. I also want to use vegetation to help satisfy the natural needs of different animals. The clouded leopard, for example, is an arboreal animal; the sign in front of its enclosure says: 'At home in the trees.' But right now, the only place our leopards have for climbing is up on top of a rock. We're going to add trees and other landscaping that will allow them to climb around like they would in the wild."

The Zoo grounds themselves offer a marvelous overall setting, with towering groves of eucalyptus trees and other exotic foliage, but Penny feels the mammal exhibits themselves can

be landscaped more effectively by adding trees, plants, and other refinements such as mounds. Like Dolan, he favors the highly developed, naturalistic exhibits seen in European zoos and he wants to create enclosures in which the type of vegetation found abroad, and capable of being grown in San Diego, will be included. "We can experiment ahead of time with cuttings from different vegetation to make sure the animals are not going to eat them, which is always a problem when you try to grow trees and plants inside an exhibit," he said.

(Even adjacent foliage can be a potential meal for animals, as founder Harry Wegeforth recalled in his memoirs: "When

A male Asian lion yawns during
a slow time on exhibit.

Two Brazilian jaguars groom
each other while on exhibit.

A confident duck glides past two river hippos.

our new elephant enclosure was being planned, I arranged for the moat to be made ten feet wide. I left on a trip, expecting the work to continue in my absence. On my return, I found the board of directors had halted it, for they thought the floor of the enclosure was too small. They had redesigned the enclosure so the moat was reduced to an eight-foot width, but they were waiting for my approval. Since I had forgotten just why I had specified ten feet in the first place, I agreed with the revised plans. As soon as the enclosure was finished, I remembered why I had specified ten feet. I had measured Empress's trunk-stretch and I learned that it was 12-½ feet from her front knees to the tip of her trunk. The eight-foot width put the palm trees planted outside the enclosure well within her reach, and she wasted no time in pulling every one of them up and devouring the tops.")

175

Above:
Chester, an Alaskan brown bear whose antics over the years have endeared him to a generation of zoogoers, cools off in his own swimming pool.

Opposite:
A North Chinese leopard hangs peacefully from a log. This species is endangered in the wild due to habitat encroachment, poaching for fur, and destruction of the big cats by livestock owners.

Right:
A Himalayan black bear takes a stroll with her playful twin cubs. The Himalayan species is often referred to as the "moon bear" because of the white crescent marking that extends across its chest.

This new exhibit for the Malayan tapirs, a severely endangered species native to the swampy forests of Burma, Sumatra, and the Malay Peninsula, provides the vegetation, running stream, and cool, shady resting areas that they seek in the wild.

Each day, hundreds of colorful and exotic birds may be seen soaring through the heights of the Tropical Rain Forest Aviary. Expanded in 1982 to accommodate a Southeast Asia theme, this is one of the world's largest walk-through aviaries.

Another of Penny's proposals consists of creating more enclosures in which compatible species—ideally, mammals, primates, birds, and reptiles alike—will share the same space. Several exhibits already have a mixture of birds and small mammals (a large group of ring-tailed lemurs, for example, are currently being exhibited with five different species of birds), and this arrangement provides a number of benefits. First, more animals can be maintained in what is essentially the same amount of space. Second, as Penny pointed out, "Mixing species very often improves the quality of the space for the animals; it's more natural, and they tend to remain more alert and involved." Third, an exhibit's educational value is enhanced when people can see a number of species living together as they might coexist in the wild.

Penny cited the giant anteater exhibit as a good example of what he envisions. "Anteaters are interesting, but not very active, so instead of wasting all this space with just one species, we're going to knock out a wall, close everything in, and add South American primates and birds. Then, we'll landscape it so it resembles the habitat they come from."

The Bird Department, in particular, stands to gain much-needed cage space and the formation of additional breeding groups if the mixed-species exhibits succeed. "We want to spread the bird population around," said Penny, "by taking some of the underutilized mammal exhibits, covering them with aviary netting, and then adding vegetation that will provide birds with plenty of safe nesting areas. However, it may take some experimenting to come up with the right birds and vegetation that the other animals won't destroy."

Unfortunately, it will take a great deal of money to accomplish these many projects. As just one example, a new home for three Malayan tapirs—which are extremely endangered in the wild—was completed in 1981 at a cost of about $130,000, and Dolan wants to build another enclosure to start a second breeding group. "This is going to cost," Penny admitted, "but it's something that is good for the animals, good for the public, and good for the Zoo. Now all we have to do is get our ideas approved by the board—and then find the money."

When it comes to putting animals out on exhibit in the coming years, important changes will have to be made by all zoos involved in the effort to sustain captive populations of endangered species. Jim Dolan stressed this ongoing challenge when he said, "If zoos are going to be serious about breeding

The African Finch Cage was re-
furbished in 1979. It was planted
with grasses and acacia trees,
and a naturalistic background
was painted to simulate an African dry veldt and provide an
attractive environment for dis-
playing colorful finches from the
southern part of Africa.

animals in captivity over the long haul, they must reorient their goals toward fewer species but a larger number of each species. So, if we're talking about four hundred or five hundred individuals of a species in captivity—which is a desirable goal—then forty or fifty zoos might have to keep ten or more individuals of that particular species. This is an incredibly difficult task, and it means that zoos can no longer afford to exhibit as many different species as possible because, given the space limitations, this would result in only one or two pairs of each being maintained."

One example of how this philosophy is already being carried out at the San Diego Zoo can be seen in Art Risser's bird collection. Responding to the fact that zoos can no longer get a steady supply of birds from the wild, he is reducing the number of different subspecies in his collection to make room for an ambitious but well-focused breeding program.

"We want to establish breeding *groups*," he said. "That means a minimum of four pairs of a certain species or subspecies. We will phase out the more common ones and concentrate on those that are more endangered, using the empty space for new family offspring and subsequent breeding pairs. We simply don't have the cages or the manpower to do this and still manage all the birds currently in our collection. Some bird fanciers are objecting to what they see as a loss of 'diversity,' but we'll still have a broad spectrum of birds that are important representatives of their genus."

Indicative of this new approach, the collection of rosellas, a colorful bird from Australia, has been pared from six representative subspecies to two: the greens, which come only from Tasmania and are the largest of the species, and the browns, which come from northern Australia and are among the smallest. "This gives us diversity not only in size but in geographic distribution," said Risser, "and we'll just concentrate on breeding those two. A lot of private aviculturists in the U.S. are already doing a good job of propagating the common types of rosellas, so it makes sense that we should focus on the ones that are difficult for them to get from Australia and also a little harder to work with in captivity."

In the new bird exhibits, as well as in those that have been modified and relandscaped, Risser has already implemented the kinds of changes that Carmi Penny also has in mind. "Whenever possible," said Risser, "our exhibits have mixtures of compatible birds that are typical of the region or habitat

Saffron finches in flight and at rest

Red-headed Gouldian finches, commonly regarded as the aristocrats of all seed-eating birds, are native to tropical northern Australia.

Colorful macaws, giants of the parrot family from Central and South America, have free movement among the tree branches in their exhibit area behind the Dryer's Flamingo Lagoon.

American flamingos "flagging." In this pre-mating courtship behavior, the males band together alternately bending their necks, swaying their heads, and flapping their wings.

In 1977, Jim Bacon's Reptile Department began upgrading exhibit quality within the confines of the venerable Reptile House. Here, Mark Hallett, a free-lance exhibit designer, transforms the large corner exhibit of the South American boa constrictor into a lush, tropical rain forest. The subsequent addition of plants, a small waterfall, and a pool then completed the effect.

Opposite:
The South American boa constrictor rests on a log in its remodeled home.

they come from. One of our new flight cages has six different species that represent a small slice of Africa, and they seem to be getting along fine. Then there's our aviary for Australian finches, which we've planted with trees, bushes, and grasses native to Australia. We've loaded it up with a variety of birds and decorated it with the same type of ecological 'furniture' they would find in the wild. People have to spend a little more time looking for the birds, but most of them appreciate the challenge and the fact that they still get to see them up close."

Ever since opening in its present location in 1922, the San Diego Zoo has exhibited animals whenever possible in open enclosures, having found that moats and other environmental barriers are a sufficient means of keeping the animals safely contained. In fact, the greater concern in recent years has been to protect the animals from the visiting public.

The Damara zebras' Zoo enclosure gives them plenty of room
for running. Of the five zebra
species, the Damaras have the
widest stripes, with a shadow
stripe sometimes appearing between the black or dark brown
ones.

Whenever possible, the Zoo exhibits its animals in open enclosures. Because giraffes are top-heavy and have an aversion to stepping down, a 30-inch-high plateau over a moat is enough to contain them.

"Considering the number of people who come to the Zoo every year [over three million], we have a very low rate of what I would term malicious mischief," said Phil Robinson, the director of veterinary services. "But occasional incidents make us shake our heads at what people will do, whatever their reasons. One morning, for example, we came to work and learned that a visitor had brought a set of darts into the Zoo and thrown them at one of our yaks. Several darts were still sticking in his skin, but fortunately he's a tough-skinned animal and he wasn't hurt. Yet the notion of anybody doing that deliberately kind of makes you feel uneasy."

A similar incident involving Devi, a young Ceylonese elephant, occurred when she was being raised in a small outdoor enclosure in the Children's Zoo. Easily accessible to the passing public, Devi liked to reach her trunk over a low barrier toward friendly-looking souls, who were urged not to feed her. One

day, a keeper was cleaning out the enclosure, her back to Devi, and when she turned around she froze in alarm finding that the elephant had curled her trunk around a lit cigar. The keeper managed to take the cigar away before it caused any harm, and then she confronted the man who had offered it to Devi. "I like animals," he tried to assure her, "and I was just curious to see what she would do with the cigar."

Despite the signs that say "Please don't feed the animals," visitors to the Zoo and Wild Animal Park still continue to do so, giving them everything from peanuts and popcorn to half-eaten sandwiches and pieces of fruit. "Public feeding is actually a form of injuring animals that, though less obvious, is still potentially fatal," said Robinson. "An animal can come down with diarrhea if somebody feeds him a bag of peanuts, or he might pick up a virus." Equally dangerous are the foreign objects such as coins, bottle caps, plastic bags, Popsicle sticks, and flashcubes that are thrown into enclosures. Many innocent animals have been injured because they were curious about these objects and ate them. A harbor seal died after swallowing several coins, and a sitatunga was lost when it ingested a stick-pin that ended up penetrating its stomach and migrating to its heart.

San Diego's policy of keeping its great apes in open enclosures, easily accessible to the public, was modified a few years back when, after a lengthy piece of detective work, it was discovered that this arrangement was proving harmful to some of the animals. As veterinarian Jane Meier reported in ZOONOOZ, the young pygmy chimps in the Ape Grotto had been suffering for several years from periodic colds which often progressed to severe pneumonia. The animals would then require hospitalization and intensive care before recovering. Since at that time there were less than forty pygmy chimps in captivity worldwide, anything that threatened their health (then as well as today) became a major cause for concern. Yet, tracing the cause of this recurrent illness proved futile, until, as Meier wrote, "Pygmy chimpanzee Louise was noticed begging from the Skyfari tram which goes over the exhibit. A passenger obligingly threw her a partially eaten apple, which she ate. Many people were also seen feeding the animals from the front of the exhibit." Blood samples then proved that a respiratory virus was being passed to the chimps by children who shared their food with the apes or spat into the exhibit. Subsequently, a mesh net was placed in front of the exhibit to help prevent public feeding, and signs were posted in the Skyfari cars to discourage people from spitting and throwing things into the enclosure. "This reduced the problem," Meier wrote, "although the pygmy chimpanzees still get pneumonia occasionally."

When animals from the wild first go on exhibit at the Zoo, curators must not only anticipate physical requirements such as diet and habitat, but also psychological needs such as the need for privacy and space. Easing an animal's transition is an important curatorial role, one that was more than fulfilled by Diane Brockman as she carefully and patiently integrated her group of red howler monkeys into the life of the Zoo. Knowing they would be skittish in front of the public and perhaps vulnerable to human viruses, she housed the group in a corner enclosure protected by glass and equipped with heaters (since winter was approaching). Having thus insured against feeding by the public, she then covered the front of the exhibit with black plastic panels. "By covering the windows," she explained, "we allowed the howlers to have only auditory contact with the public until they adjusted to their new quarters. After several weeks, we removed a panel from one of the windows, enabling the howlers to become acclimated to the public but with plenty of room to still hide from that constant scrutiny. Eventually we cleared both windows."

Once a group of animals has been put on exhibit, the keepers then look for signs that being on display all day is adversely affecting the group or an individual within the group. Such clues might include overly aggressive or withdrawn behavior, a refusal to eat, a loss of weight, or a lack of, or decline in, sexual activity and reproductive success. When such signs begin to appear, the habitat is modified—if possible—or the animals are taken off exhibit.

The experience of the Zoo's group of douc langurs, a hauntingly beautiful and endangered animal that arrived from the wild in 1968, provides a good case in point. Although the group at first seemed to be faring reasonably well in captivity, with youngsters being born regularly, stress-related symptoms began to appear in the late 1970s.

"They became terribly upset when crowds gathered in front of their enclosures and eventually they began to exhibit nervous behaviors," said Brockman. "When two of them died, the necropsies revealed that both had stomach ulcers. There is no doubt that the ulcers were stress-related, for the psychological and emotional delicacy of douc langurs is really striking. When you look at one of these animals, he will stare back or turn away. If he stares back, it means he's challenging you. When he opens his mouth in what seems to be a big yawn, he is making the maximum challenge. If he turns away, it means he's becoming subordinate to you. So you can imagine the effect of fifteen, twenty, or thirty people standing in front of the enclosure staring at a douc. That represents fifteen, twenty, or thirty threats or challenges. Actually, it's a challenge or a threat to *any* monkey when you stare and make eye-to-eye contact, but few people realize how significant that one unobtrusive behavior is, especially to such a highly sensitive animal as the douc langur."

When it became obvious that the doucs were unable to cope with large crowds, they were moved to private quarters. They have since been put back on public view in a climate-controlled enclosure in the Heart of the Zoo, but this time, under more favorable circumstances. "We didn't want to deprive people of appreciating the elegance and beauty of these animals," Brockman noted, "but we've designed an exhibit that will also give the doucs an opportunity to get out of sight, away from people and from each other."

The douc langurs point up a crucial dilemma that is faced by all urban zoos: what to do with those endangered species that have display value and also desperately need to have their numbers increased in captivity, but cannot be displayed and bred simultaneously? Not surprisingly, many animals breed better when they have privacy, and not simply at night when the zoo is closed. If they are kept on permanent display, their reproductive activity declines, and sometimes even ceases.

One solution, says Diane Brockman, is to have off-exhibit areas for those species which obviously need more privacy than is available on public display (and not necessarily more living space, which is often the case for the larger mammals), but to keep some members of the species on exhibit for the public's enjoyment and education. "My own personal philosophy," said Brockman, "is that for every species on exhibit, you should have animals off exhibit. Ideally, this enables you to have a large

The exquisite-looking douc langur is rarely kept in zoological collections (fewer than forty animals exist in captivity worldwide) and is endangered in its geographic range—the war-torn jungles of Vietnam, Laos, and Cambodia.

enough group of animals to maintain genetic viability. You can't keep all your animals on exhibit if you plan to do justice to the species."

Carrying out this theme, Brockman's department now has the Primate Propagation Center, a series of enclosures on a secluded hillside behind the Zoo hospital. This private compound will be invaluable in helping the Zoo to become as self-sufficient as possible in terms of propagating all the primates that it wishes to house. Successful breeding groups here will allow Brockman to continuously rotate animals on and off exhibit as the need arises, while maintaining large overall groups of primates. "The animals we have on exhibit will be for education," she said, "and if we get babies, great. But the Primate Propagation Center will be for serious reproductive efforts."

The Bird Department instituted a similar program in 1980, when it opened the Avian Propagation Center (also adjacent to the hospital). "This facility represents a new era of captive bird management and reproduction," noted Art Risser.

"Even though our efforts in cage modernization are directed toward providing seclusion for nesting birds, incubation failures do take place," he said. "And there's always the danger that when young birds are startled before they have adjusted to everyday disturbances around the enclosure, chick mortality will occur." To eliminate these risks, especially for the endangered bird species, eggs are removed from the nest and then placed in artificial incubators at the Avian Propagation Center. Removing the eggs like this can also provide a stimulus for the female to deposit more eggs. Once the baby birds are old enough, they are sent to other institutions, to private aviculturists, or into the Zoo's own display enclosures. (During the 1982 season, more than eight hundred hatchlings of sixty species—including Darwin's rheas, Bulwer's pheasants, ocellated turkeys, and masked bobwhite quails—were successfully incubated here.)

The Avian Propagation Center also includes over eighty breeding cages of varying sizes to serve as off-display homes for successful breeding pairs and for difficult or temperamental birds.

At the Wild Animal Park, where most of the over one hundred species live in mixed groups in spacious exhibits, the field staff of about twenty keepers is continually looking for

In a typical scene at the Park, different species such as giraffes and Cape buffalo peacefully intermingle.

Giraffes and a black rhino survey the East Africa exhibit from near Pumzika Point, just off the Kilimanjaro Hiking Trail.

ways to make the environment as natural as possible for the resident animals.

When Carmi Penny was working at the Park, he took a visitor for a drive through the East Africa exhibit, which at the time contained eighteen different species and over two hundred individual animals. Looking down from a favorite hillside observation point, he commented, "We could have left this as a sterile exhibit with nothing in it but animals, and they would have survived all right. Instead, we chose to create an exhibit that caters to each species living here, because there's a big difference between the raw needs of an animal and its natural needs."

Park curator Larry Killmar concurred, pointing out the subtle things that make an animal feel at home—"like providing browse trees instead of simply laying the browse on the ground. The natural browsers, like giraffes, gerenuks, elands, and kudus, can make the adjustment, but they're much happier reaching up to eat than having to bend down all the time.

A Northern gerenuk dines on acacia browse hung from a tree at the Park. These giraffe-necked antelope (unrelated to giraffes) pluck off the leaves with their long upper lips and tongues.

The wire mesh that protects many of the Park's trees from destruction by the resident animals also serves as a convenient scratching post for the giraffes.

Giraffes enjoy eating acacia branches tied to a tree.

An Afghan urial herd at the top of Mountain Habitat—a steep, rocky hillside area across from the Asian Swamp exhibit

Another thing we do is leave tree stumps, so that the rhinos can rub their hides, and the other animals can satisfy territorial instincts by scenting their areas with urine. When we can help meet these natural needs, we make it much easier for them to get along with one another."

Although the Park averages only about ten inches of rain a year, most visitors—aesthetically, at least—would prefer to see the hills and valleys carpeted with grass. In coming years, they will get their wish, for a program has been instituted to irrigate and thus transform nearly all the Park grounds. Beautification, however, was not the motivating force behind these plans. The Park must irrigate in order to maintain a constant food source and, more importantly, to lessen the problem of erosion. The porous, crushed granite soil erodes easily, creating dangerous ditches and gullies for the animals, while sending silt down into the small lakes in the East Africa and South Africa exhibits.

"All the native ground cover and vegetation was destroyed by the animals the first two years they were out here," Killmar noted, "so these hills would eventually erode away if we simply let nature take its course. Yet, we can't ignore animal preferences, so we have to compromise. The addax, for example,

Addax, which are native to the Sahara Desert, are at home in the North Africa exhibit, one of the Park's more barren areas. Though few addax survive in the wild today, they are reproducing well in captivity.

These three Formosan sika deer in the Asian Swamp exhibit represent a species that is extinct in the wild, but faring well in captivity.

Kenya impala, shown here in flight across a hillside in the East Africa exhibit, are another species that has flourished at the Park.

An Indian rhino bathes in the stream that runs through the Asian Plains exhibit. In the wild, Indian rhinos bathe daily and are also fond of wallowing in the mud.

The barasingha, or swamp deer, is an aquatic animal and can usually be found near the pond or stream in the Asian Plains exhibit.

come from a desert environment and they would be quite at home if we just left their entire exhibit [North Africa] as dry as possible. But erosion makes it a dangerous area for babies of other species, which means we must grass over the hillsides. The valleys and draws, though, will be left in their natural state so that animals who dislike grass or wet areas can still retreat to an area where they won't feel stressed. In spite of the risks, we'll also retain suitably rough terrain for certain animals to hide their babies. The mothers in certain species need a place to hide or 'tuck' their babies for several weeks after birth, and if we didn't provide areas that satisfied these anti-predator instincts, we could produce aberrant behavior.

"Sure these exhibits would look 'beautiful' covered entirely by grass, but we'd be negligent if we didn't consider the practical needs of animals like the zebra, who need an area to dust themselves [mostly as a deterrent to parasites such as fleas]; if we didn't provide this, they would do something else and very likely cause problems for another group of animals as they displaced their frustration. We also maintain barren areas that are used by bachelor groups [males who have been excluded from the main herd]. We purposely don't enhance these areas, with trees or whatever, because we don't want to attract other groups. We want to give the loners a place to run to, where they can basically avoid both trouble and interaction with other animals."

Carmi Penny also cited the impala, which is considered a transition-zone animal—one who prefers to spend time in the intermediate area between a dry zone and a moist one. "We've created a transition zone by purposely keeping some of these hills dry (foregoing the grass we've started on other hills) and by maintaining dry areas between the hills that lead down to the moist area along the stream [which runs year-round through the exhibit]. Then, there are animals like the sitatunga which need places to go where they can get away from the other species. The sitatunga is the most aquatic of all the antelopes and it likes to hide along the stream and down around the lake at the lower end of the exhibit. By catering to needs like this, it stands to reason that our reproduction rate will be much higher than if we had left the exhibits unchanged."

Another exhibiting conflict at the Park involves the Asian Swamp, a heavily irrigated, 35-acre enclosure in which numerous hiding places have been provided for the animals, mostly exotic deer and goats. "There's a philosophical problem we're always wrestling with here," Killmar explained. "One group within the Society says, 'You've got to show the public everything they want because they're paying the bills.' But

Two views of Sagar Tal, the landscaped home for Hanuman langurs at the Park. This exhibit is named for a remote spot in India where gods are said to mingle with animals. Hanumans are considered sacred in India, where they are associated with the Hindu god Hanuman, but they are still endangered there because human overcrowding is reducing the amount of suitable habitat.

The Park's monorail ride offers a clear view of the Gorilla Grotto. Surrounding trees have grown considerably since this photograph was taken in 1976.

This island in the remodeled pond at the lower end of the East Africa exhibit houses a family of colobus monkeys.

another element argues, 'This is also an animal reserve out here and we have to let the animals have their private areas, away from public view, if we expect to maximize reproduction.' These views tend to clash in this exhibit. A lot of people complain because they have a hard time seeing the animals from the monorail. But this exhibit functions wonderfully for the animals, and we can never overlook that."

When the two small lakes at the Park were dredged and expanded in 1982, Killmar knew this expensive facelift would benefit the Park, but he worried that the changes might adversely affect the animals. "As logical as this construction might seem on the surface," he said, "it required a lot of thinking before we decided to go ahead with it." After both lakes were drained and dredged, the rich silt was hauled into adjoining valleys where mounds and knolls were created, later to be covered with grass. This renovation not only doubled the Park's water-holding capacity during the rainy season, thus reducing its water bills, it also transformed two flat, relatively lifeless basins into an eye-pleasing sight for visitors passing by on the monorail.

"This will undoubtedly attract more animal activity down here by providing a better water source," said Killmar, "and the water will be deeper for those animals who like to wade out in hot weather—like some of the antelopes who stand chest deep in the water to cool down. The rhinos will also enjoy coming down and wallowing in the mud. However, as nice as the new landscaping might look to the public, we might just be 180 degrees off from what most of the other animals actually require. The animals who used to stay down closer to the lakes when the area was pretty dry and barren may not like all this grass underfoot, and they could decide to move away toward the back of the exhibit. This in turn could create a stress factor because the animals that are currently happy back there will be crowded, and the competition for space could provoke a lot of fighting between species and some of our animals might stop breeding."

Fortunately, Killmar's fears were not borne out. The existing animals adjusted without incident and were joined by new neighbors: families of colobus and grivet monkeys on two of the three islands and greater numbers of waterfowl.

FEEDING
THE ANIMALS

S tarting at about six o'clock every morning, when the air is filled with the sound of waking animals, a driver heads out from the Zoo's food warehouse, his flatbed truck loaded with hay, grains, food pellets, horsemeat, fish, and fresh fruit and vegetables. By about seven-thirty he has made his deliveries to the various feeding centers around the Zoo—the Reptile House, the monkey yard, the bird yard, the great ape enclosures, the mammal quarters, the hospital, and the Children's Zoo—and the keepers then begin to prepare the morning meals.

In the bird yard kitchen, for example, keepers chop and dice the fruits and vegetables, apportion the mixture into shallow feeding pans and then distribute these to each cage. "The basic daily diet is pretty much the same for all the birds," said general curator Art Risser, "but there's plenty of variety in each tray, so the birds always have a choice." The trays include such items as carrots, greens, tomatoes, bananas, apples, papayas, oranges, blueberries, raisins, and dog chow biscuits enriched with vitamins. Certain birds also receive crickets, mealworms, sunflower seeds, game-bird pellets, and a ground meat concoction.

A different type of breakfast is fed to the flamingos, who are among the pickiest eaters at the Zoo. In the wild, they eat crustaceans every day which keeps their plumage pink (they are actually gray as fledglings), but such a diet would be too costly for the Zoo to maintain—especially for a group of twenty to thirty birds—so a complex, substitute diet has been formulated instead. Every morning, a keeper fills a ten-gallon blender with the following ingredients: two kinds of shrimp (pink and white), salmon, fish, shrimp meal, bone meal, alfalfa meal, salt, cooked grains (wheat, millet, and rice), beet tops, grated carrots, and two teaspoons of roxanthin, a red dye powder. He adds water, turns on the blender, and after filling two large buckets with the mixture, he then transfers the food into metal pans located in Flamingo Lagoon.

Meanwhile, in the adjacent monkey yard, keepers are preparing the morning meal for their roughly 125 residents. Nearly all the monkeys receive high-protein monkey chow biscuits, a commercially prepared food, while the leaf-eating species also receive branches of hibiscus and eugenia to supplement their diets. In the afternoon, all are given chopped-up fruits and vegetables along with monkey chow biscuits that have been moistened and supplemented with raisins, a protein pow-

A forage warehouse worker sorts through the fresh fruit and vegetables to be distributed to many of the Zoo's animals.

An American flamingo and her chick, beak to beak at feeding time. This youngster will have a succession of coats, finally acquiring its adult coloration and plumage at about a year of age.

Keeper Susie Ellis prepares food trays for the birds.

Hanuman langurs pick through
assorted pieces of fruits and vegetables at the Park.

Keeper Jane Jacobson feeds four
of the ring-tailed lemurs in her
care from a metal tray.

der, and vitamin oil. "We try to emphasize the vegetables," said curator Diane Brockman, "because if we feed them too many bananas—which they love—they'll fill up on bananas and skip what's better for them. Too much fruit can also cause a loose stool problem."

Since the primates will maintain their social ranking at feeding time if there is only one feeding station—the dominant male eating first, followed by the older females and then the juveniles—food pans are scattered throughout their enclosures. With this arrangement the subordinate members of the group are assured of getting enough to eat, while the dominant animals are discouraged from overeating. While Brockman prefers to feed the monkeys a natural diet whenever possible, she realizes that the specially prepared monkey chow mixture insures a more nutritious diet for each of the primates.

Feeding the hoofed stock is a rather straightforward process, since nearly all of them eat hay and "The Complete San Diego Zoo Pellet," a scientifically developed food that provides them with their basic nutritional requirements. The carnivores—lions, leopards, tigers, polar bears, wolves, and Tasmanian devils—receive hunks of horsemeat and Zupreem (a ground meat concoction). "Many zoos used to make a big mistake by feeding carnivores an exclusively muscle-meat diet," said veterinarian Phil Robinson. "We add vitamins and a calcium supplement, since muscle meats, all by themselves, have imbalances of calcium and phosphorous that can lead to rickets. A soft meat diet like this can also lead to buildup of plaque that develops into periodontal disease, so once a week the carnivores are given nothing but oxtails or other types of bones to chew. This keeps their teeth in good condition and provides them with something different to do at mealtime."

Although a freshly killed horse or other domestic animal would give the carnivores a more appetizing and naturalistic meal than the five-pound loaves of Zupreem, providing them with this would be both uneconomical and controversial. Equally important, it could very well prove harmful. "If we fed the lions or tigers an entire dead horse that happened to have parasites," said Robinson, "our animals would in turn get those parasites. So, we eliminate that risk, plus we can add vitamin and mineral supplements, gauge how much an individual animal is actually eating, and know that a subordinate animal within a group is not getting stuck with a leftover carcass."

There are over four thousand mouths to feed at the Zoo—at an average daily cost of about 35 cents each—but not all of them need to be fed every day. This is especially true of the reptiles, whose individual feeding times fluctuate, depending on their metabolism and on the time of year. "The Burmese pythons are the best eaters," said head keeper Tom Schultz. "They go through ten rats at a time about every two weeks, and they'd certainly eat more if we offered it to them, but we have to watch their weight; you'll shorten a large constrictor's life if you feed him too much." Yet, he pointed out, a healthy python can also go without food for three months or more and show no signs of distress.

"We once had a western diamondback rattler who went for fifteen months without eating, and he showed little loss in weight or body tone," Schultz recalled. "We tried everything—rabbits, ground squirrels, pigeons, even mackerel—until one day he decided to sample one of the rats we had been putting in his cage. After that, the snake ate every week for years and years."

One of the most popular animals at the Zoo in the mid-1920s was a 20-foot long reticulated python named Diablo, who grew famous due to his refusal to eat. He was an extremely stubborn snake, and would not eat anything, no matter how tempting it might have been to other pythons. To prevent starvation, Harry Wegeforth decided that Diablo should be force-fed, and he devised a machine for the purpose that was similar to those used for stuffing sausages. Eleven men were needed to hold the snake while it was being fed, and this monthly spectacle soon became so popular that Wegeforth, smelling profit, planned the feedings at convenient times, published the schedule in the newspaper, and then charged five cents' admission. Somehow Diablo lived on like this for nearly six years.

"Force-feeding Diablo was good PR, but bad management practice," said today's reptile curator, Jim Bacon. "It's fairly remarkable that he put up with that stuff for so long without getting an infected throat. Force-feeding an adult snake is a technique herpetologists turn to as a last resort, because usually when an adult snake won't eat, there's a good reason—it is sick, and is very often going to die anyway. However, we often have to force-feed newly born reptiles because a significant number of them don't know what the front end is all about at first. This is true in the wild as well. If we're lucky,

This two-foot-long African egg-eating snake is harmless, unless you happen to be an egg. Here, a hungry snake has found an egg that is about two inches in diameter—roughly four times the size of its own head.

The snake opens its mouth as it prepares to swallow the egg. Its upper and lower jawbones are loosely connected to one another by stretchy ligaments. Special gums, which are like suction cups, enable the snake to hold on to the slick egg without letting it slip.

The skin around the snake's mouth stretches to make way for the egg. Composed of pleated folds of skin, the mouth expands much in the same way that an accordion does.

Slowly the egg slides down the snake's throat. Sharp points on the snake's backbone crack the egg before it reaches the stomach.

The snake then twists and turns. This motion crushes the shell, forcing the contents of the egg into the stomach.

The snake twists and turns some more, finally regurgitating the empty eggshell.

143
Passmore
San Diego

Upwards of eleven men were needed to force-feed Diablo, a 20-foot-long python who refused to eat. This "event" drew such large crowds in the mid-1920s that it was used as a device to raise money for the Zoo.

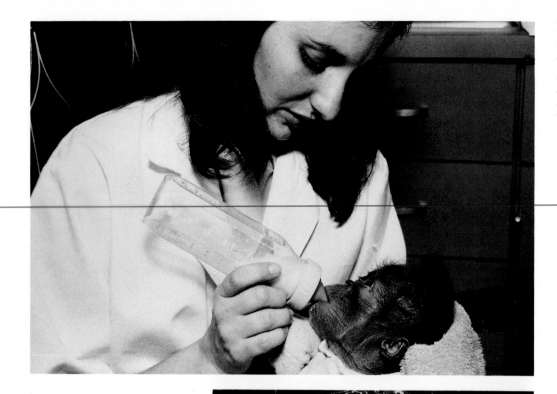

Bo, the offspring of Sumatran orangutans Bubbles and Otis, was fed human infant formula every two hours during her first weeks at the Starkey Primate Nursery.

An aardvark baby receives its bottle-feeding. Aardvarks, a pig-sized mammal, are found throughout most of Africa south of the Sahara.

Gumby, a Leadbeater's cockatoo, eats formula from a spoon.
Hand-rearing birds is a difficult,
lengthy process because frequent feedings are required.

though, one meal will get a youngster's appetite working well
enough so that it will feed naturally the next time it is offered
food."

At the Zoo and the Wild Animal Park, when babies are
abandoned or rejected by their mother, are not nursing properly, or appear to be sick or injured, keepers pull them for hand-
raising in specially designed animal nurseries.

Most of the hoofed stock and primate babies—from Mhorr
gazelles to pygmy chimps—are bottle-fed, using formulas
worked out by the veterinarians and the nursery staffs. In the
Zoo's Starkey Primate Nursery, for example, Lisa and Lock,
twin orangutans, were fed a fortified infant formula and junior
baby food with cereal or oatmeal added. Toui-San, a clouded
leopard, received kitten milk replacer and Zupreem. And a
four-month-old aardvark ate a meat-base formula with squash
and milk added, later supplemented with hard-boiled egg yolks
and wheat hearts, a dry cereal.

Over the years, a great variety of newborns at the Park—
including white rhinos, giraffes, water buffalo, and gorillas—
have been hand-raised at the Animal Care Center. In late spring

and summer, upwards of thirty to forty babies might be on
bottles at any given time, since nearly all the offspring of such
prolific species as blackbuck and axis deer are automatically
pulled for hand-raising at birth (thus bypassing the problem of
having to capture them in an open exhibit when, later, it comes
time for them to be shipped to another facility). Terry Blakes-
ley, the keeper in charge of the Animal Care Center, described
the initial hand-raising process as follows:

*When a baby comes in from the field, we already know what kind of
formula it's going to receive, through past experience with the species.
We determine how much formula it should get by its weight and we
usually use either a powdered milk formula, canned goat's milk and
water, or cow's milk and water. These formulas are simple to prepare;
they're relatively inexpensive, and they work well, so we don't have to
worry about exotic and expensive formulas.*

*If a baby is brought in before it has nursed from its mother, it will
usually nurse from rubber nipples right away or within a day, and not
know the difference. But if it has nursed from its mother, we sometimes
have a terrible time. Some of these babies will go for days without
eating because they're waiting for mom to come by and get them. We
try all sorts of ways to get them to take the bottle—stand them up, sit
them down, use different-shaped nipples, try different formulas, make
different sounds, pat them in different places, and so on. Just putting the
nipple in their mouth is not enough, nor does it matter that they're close
to starvation. We've lost some babies who never would nurse. It's as if
they have a switch inside that must be turned on to trigger the nursing
instinct. Then when they suddenly do decide to nurse, whatever you
were doing at that moment becomes the way it is fed the next time, and
the other keepers are told: "He ate when I did this, this, and this." Very
often that becomes the only way he will eat and you have to go through
the same routine every time, for weeks.*

*Blackbucks can be especially stubborn, but one trick that occasionally
works is to take them out to be with the older blackbucks in the Petting
Kraal. Sometimes the youngster will pick one out that he thinks is his
mother and will start looking underneath for the nipple, at which point
we try to get the bottle under there and into his mouth while he's
searching.*

*We've also learned, by watching mothers nudge their babies out in
the field, that if we stimulate a baby on the rump, this quite often starts
the nursing reflex. Vocalizing like the mother also helps, since it triggers
this natural instinct. We learn these sounds by listening to the babies
and to the older animals that we are caring for in here.*

When a pair of endangered Andean condors, Andy and Elizabeth, laid their first egg in 1981, Zoo keepers removed the egg for artificial incubation at the Avian Propagation Center, where it hatched two months later. Here, the chick, named Rodan, is being fed with puppets specially designed to look like real condor parents. Though time-consuming, this technique helped the baby imprint on birds rather than humans.

When Rodan was about six months old, he was moved to the Park's new off-exhibit aviary, where he shares this flight cage with a parent-raised condor chick from the Zoo. Eventually, the Zoo hopes to reintroduce these birds to their native wild habitat in Peru.

We feed the orphaned hoofed-stock babies every two hours, from 6:00 A.M. to 6:00 P.M. for a week—and let them sleep all night. Then we drop the feedings down to every three hours. By the time they're a month old, they're feeding three times a day and we leave them on that schedule but increase the amount for another month. Most of the animals, unless they're exceptionally large, are weaned by the time they're three months old.

Through experience, scientific research, and good old-fashioned trial and error, Zoo and Wild Animal Park curators and veterinarians have developed diets that keep every animal as well-nourished as possible. "Healthy animals are capable of, and interested in, reproduction," Phil Robinson wrote in ZOONOOZ. "Animals that are sick or in suboptimal health do not reproduce well, if at all." He pointed out that subtle factors related to nutrition and dental health are now known to exert a significant influence not only on reproductive success, but on lifespans as well. Thus, though a diet is initially worked out by drawing on an animal's known food preferences in the wild and the nutritional requirements of related domestic or captive species, it will usually continue to evolve in response to firsthand experience and research findings. This approach has become more prevalent in recent years as the Zoo and the Wild Animal Park have increasingly come to rely upon the expertise of Michigan State's Dr. Duane Ullrey, a well-known animal nutritionist. He uses laboratory analysis to carry out special nutritional studies and periodically comes to San Diego to evaluate various diets.

"Before purchasing many of our products," said Phil Robinson, "we have Duane review the ingredients to determine which ones are the most desirable. We also want to make sure that the diet we're feeding certain groups of animals is appropriate. In many cases, we really don't know specifically what an animal *needs*, as opposed to what it seems to prefer. Like people, many animals in captivity fail to make intelligent selections about what's proper and what's improper as far as diet goes. There's research to show, for instance, that monkeys and lemurs will not select the nutritionally best diet but will go for the more palatable one."

When the Zoo acquires a new species from the wild, the challenge—especially with primates—is to come up with a nutritious diet that the animals will eat. This was a particular concern when the large group of wild-caught red howlers ar-

Whenever possible, of course, Zoo keepers allow nature to take its course. Here, a toco toucan reaches into the nest to feed its young, the first of this species to be raised at the Zoo. The nest was located in a large, hollow palm log in the Scripps Flight Cage, the birds' exhibit area.

Once these three chicks were hatched, the parents busily fed them for forty-three days. Keepers then removed the chicks, fearing that they might be injured by other birds once they left the nest.

The three toco toucans as juveniles

rived at the Zoo in 1981. These leaf-eating monkeys have delicate appetites, and curator Diane Brockman knew their survival depended on how quickly they could adjust to a captive diet that had to include more than just foliage. She started them off on monkey chow biscuits soaked in water, with bananas mashed in. They liked this and it supplied their basic nutritional needs, but as Brockman mentioned, "When you're working with a finicky species like this, you can never let their diet remain static." So, she experimented with different foods and borrowed a black howler diet from the Riverbanks Zoo in South Carolina, eventually ending up with a menu that was complex and expensive—but popular with her diners. In the morning, the howlers would get a monkey chow mixture that had been soaked in evaporated milk and tea, and fortified with vitamins, a vanilla-flavored high protein powder, honey, and raisins. This feeding was supplemented with cup-of-gold leaves, eugenia leaves, and hibiscus leaves. The afternoon meal consisted of more of the monkey chow mixture, two cups of yogurt (banana and peach flavors), and an assortment of fruit and vegetables cut up into small pieces.

All the animals in the Zoo have their meals and their overall diets closely monitored, for nutritional as well as weight-watching purposes. In the wild, these animals would be spending most of their waking hours hunting for food and covering their territory. But since they live in confined areas at the Zoo, and nobody goes hungry, obesity can become a problem. If an animal does become overweight, he is placed on a special diet until he returns to his desired weight. Such was the case for the Zoo's Komodo monitor male, a voracious eater whose feedings had to be cut back in frequency and quantity when his weight climbed past 220 pounds. In order to keep his weight at a svelte 190, his weekly diet was limited to one pigeon, three or four rats, and one small rabbit—about one-third the amount he had formerly been given.

Among the primates, particular attention is given to the gorillas and the orangutans, who are less inclined to be phys-

Mandrill mother and her baby out on exhibit

Many animals in captivity need occupational food to keep them busy and alert. Gorillas, like Jim here, enjoy picking apart clumps of Zoo-grown grass or munching on acacia branches.

ically active as they grow older but who nevertheless retain huge appetites. "Obesity in captive apes is a problem," said keeper Gale Foland. "And with a guy like Otis [the patriarch of the Sumatran orangs], it's an honest temptation to want to feed him too much, because he looks forward to it so much. There's nothing he'd rather do than eat."

Food at the Zoo is also looked upon in terms of psychology. To combat boredom, and often to supplement prepared diets, the animals are frequently provided browse, insects, mealworms, and other "occupational" foods to keep them busy and alert. As former horticulturist Ernie Chew pointed out, some of the leaf-eating monkeys get eugenia and hibiscus leaves and blossoms to nibble on and pull apart. Other animals take the browse apart, stripping leaves from branches, pulling bark from stems, and picking out seeds. The gorillas prefer to simply play with large pieces of bamboo, banana plants, acacia branches, and palm fronds. The Tahitian lories, meanwhile,

are given branches of blossoming eucalyptus trees and the flowered stalks of palm trees so they can spend time seeking out pollen, one of their natural foods in the wild.

At the Wild Animal Park, the daily challenge of feeding the animals in the open range areas is entrusted to teams of field keepers working from flatbed trucks. The keepers arrive at the Park between six and six-thirty in the morning, meeting in front of a trailer which serves as headquarters for curator Larry Killmar, who is in charge of day-to-day field operations. After they discuss any special projects that need attention that morning, the keepers drive to the food warehouses, load their trucks, and then fan out to their respective exhibits. (The keepers rotate between the "feed run" crew—which feeds and inventories all the animals by taking a daily nose count—and the "bull" crew, which is responsible for cleanup and maintenance.)

Since the Park's large herd of addax can be dangerously aggressive when feeding begins, keepers stay in their truck as they unload the morning's supply of hay.

Przewalski's horses eat hay from one of the feeders located in all the field exhibits at the Park.

A giraffe bends down to share a feeding log with an unintimidated slender-horned gazelle.

When keepers head for the Asian Plains exhibit, for example, their truck is loaded with five bales of hay (three of oats, and one each of alfalfa and Sudan grass), large sacks of alfalfa pellets and high-protein herbivore pellets, and three tubs of goodies for the Indian rhinos. (Nearly all the animals in this exhibit are grazers and they satisfy much of their appetite by eating grass.) The hay and pellets are distributed to about fifteen different feed stations, which are strategically located throughout the exhibit in order to minimize competition among the eleven species that live there and to allow for public viewing from the monorail. Each station is monitored and if a group of animals suddenly moves to a new feeder location, to the detriment of another species, an additional feeder is usually built nearby. In the South Africa exhibit, for example, a special feeding station had to be built for the greater kudu (a member of the antelope family), for they were being excluded from their fair share by more aggressive animals. "Since the kudu are highly selective eaters and extremely meek," Killmar explained, "we built the shelter in such a way that only smaller animals could enter, through gaps in the structure. Hanging the kudu's browse inside also kept it a little fresher and more palatable in hot weather."

The tubs for the Indian rhinos contain carrots, yams, apples, oranges, and omaline (an oat and molasses horse feed). "Nutritionally, this stuff is unimportant," keeper Rick Barongi noted. "They certainly wouldn't eat it in the wild, but this was part of their original diet at the Park and they really love it. This has helped us develop a rapport with them; they are more trusting of us when they see us come out with the tubs, and we can manipulate them more easily. If we want to get an 8,000-pound rhino like Lasai to do something—like cooperate with the visiting press—we just show him the tub and he'll follow it anywhere."

Lasai receives the first tub, well away from Jaipuri and their two offspring, Gainda and Pandu. Immediately, he is joined by a wapiti stag, a friendly but rather brazen neighbor who has acquired a taste for these morning morsels and who has learned to take advantage of Lasai's friendly nature to steal from his tub. The wapiti has an enormous rack of antlers, and though Lasai is not intimidated as he noses around in the tub, he allows the wapiti an opening. The stag's head quickly darts in to snap up a carrot. Knowing that Lasai is not going to toss his head around in order to keep the tub all to himself, the wapiti keeps on selecting his share of goodies. Meanwhile, as Jaipuri works on her tub, a female barasingha deer comes over to pay a visit, as is her daily habit. "She doesn't have antlers," said Barongi, "but she's a smart old gal and she has worked out a strategy that outsmarts the rhinos. She waits until Jaipuri lifts her head to chew, then quickly seizes a piece of food and moves away to eat it. Then she comes back and waits next to Jaipuri until the rhino raises her head again." This interplay goes on every day between the rhinos and the deer. They've worked out the ground rules and only rarely do they get angry with one another.

A group of addra gazelles at the Park, grazing on one of the hillsides in their exhibit

VETERINARY CARE

When she's anticipating a "normal" day at the Zoo, veterinarian Jane Meier arrives for work at eight in the morning. She first visits any hospitalized animals who need examining, such as those recovering from surgery or fighting an illness. Then she meets with the other veterinarians on duty and they review a daily checklist which includes animals that need treatment, are under close observation for a suspected medical problem, or have had prescriptions dispensed to them. "We go over this list and update each other," said Meier, "and then we decide [if a decision wasn't made the day before] who will handle the various cases. We often have to work together on an involved surgery, which will generally consume most of the morning by the time we set up, get the animal anesthetized, do the surgery, finish up, revive the animal, and then write our report."

If no urgent surgery is required, the veterinarians begin their daily rounds. "We each cover regular areas, such as the monkey yard, the bird yard, the Reptile House, the nurseries, the Koala House, and the off-exhibit breeding pads, so that we stay in touch with the keepers and the animals," said Meier. "Plus, we visit places where we're monitoring a particular animal or treating it on the grounds. We like to get as much of this work done before the Zoo opens [at nine o'clock], so that we don't interfere with the public and they don't interfere with us."

After these morning rounds have been completed, the vets tend to their routine hospital work, which consists of performing minor surgeries, giving medical treatment, and examining animals in quarantine. Quarantined animals spend approximately thirty days at the hospital, during which time the vets give them physical examinations, check them for parasites, vaccinate them when necessary, give them identification tattoos, and make sure they're adapting to their diets.

Most afternoons are spent on an equally varied assortment of projects. "We might have a meeting with a curator and several keepers to discuss a particular husbandry problem or to plan a new long-range program," said Phil Robinson, the director of veterinary services. "Or, we might be focusing on a nutrition study when suddenly an animal breaks its leg and we have to drop everything we're doing—then catch up later."

Jane Meier, a graduate of Purdue University, joined the Zoo staff as an associate veterinarian in 1976. "Zoo medicine is an

Diana, the first giant anteater ever born at the Zoo, had to be raised in the Children's Zoo nursery when her mother refused to care for her—the most common problem necessitating hand-raising.

Hand-raised nursery primates such as Leslie, a pygmy chimp, and Sarah, an orangutan, are grouped together whenever possible. The apes enjoy playing together and this socialization helps prepare them for the day when they will join their respective troops out on exhibit.

incredibly broad field," she noted, "and I sometimes feel we're the ultimate general practitioners. We deal with the same sort of problems seen in people hospitals—fractures, traumas, heart disease, ulcers, depression, cancer, pneumonia, old age, periodontal disease, and so on—but we must treat many species of patients with varied anatomies and physiologies." In her career at the Zoo, for example, she has given daily insulin injections to ring-tailed lemurs with diabetes mellitus, helped repair lacerations on a Galápagos tortoise, treated a Himalayan black bear for an abscess resulting from a splinter in his paw, done a caesarean section on a Gaboon viper, and performed a host of similar duties. She has also had to cope with emergencies that were never covered back in medical school.

One such incident occurred when Sumithi, a Ceylonese elephant, became wedged upside down in the moat surrounding the elephant enclosure—the result of either an accidental fall or a rival's well-timed shove. Most of the keepers had already gone home, but Meier and keeper Ken Willingham were quickly on the scene organizing a rescue effort, for they realized that an elephant in this position usually has no more than about an hour to live. (An inverted elephant is in danger of suffocating or hemorrhaging due to insufficient amounts of air reaching the lungs or insufficient amounts of blood reaching the heart.) Meier had one keeper try to soothe the elephant while another was sent to get oxygen and tranquil-

izing equipment should the need for them arise. A food service worker was sent to get bales of straw, and security personnel were told to keep back a crowd that had been gathering ever since the distress cries of the elephant first began to reverberate throughout the Zoo.

"The most difficult part," Meier recalled, "was knowing that with the right equipment—a derrick, for instance—getting Sumithi upright would have been a fairly simple procedure. We didn't have a derrick, and we didn't have much time. Furthermore, I didn't know whether any bones had been broken and, therefore, whether she'd be able to help herself up once we got her into a sitting position." Such thoughts were pushed to the back of her mind as Meier, intending to have the elephant pulled out of the moat, ordered one end of a rope tied safely around Sumithi's neck and the other end attached to another elephant in the enclosure. It was a good plan, but the cooperating elephant simply did not have the strength to do the job.

Next, Willingham's truck was positioned right outside the enclosure wall, and the end of the rope was tied to its trailer hitch. Sumithi was inched up a little, but when the truck's tires began to spin, Meier knew she needed something with better traction and greater power. She remembered that a forklift was somewhere on the grounds, so one of the keepers rushed off to find it. Thirty minutes had already slipped by,

Freddie, a hand-raised mandrill

Squirrel monkey babies enjoy their "tree hole" nest in the Children's Zoo nursery.

Fenwick, a common marmoset, had a swollen finger that required treatment by a Park veterinarian.

but, fortunately, the machine arrived in time. "The forklift saved the day," said Meier. "We used it to pull Sumithi into a sitting position so she was able to stand on her own and climb out of the moat using the straw bales that had been stacked into a ramp."

Although the vets must devote a certain amount of time to emergencies such as this, and to the day-to-day run of injuries and illnesses that occur, they—in cooperation with the keepers—try to spend as much time as possible on preventive medicine. "It's a lot easier to keep animals from getting sick than it is to deal with the problem once it occurs," Meier noted. "Most of our patients don't appreciate direct contact as we try to make a diagnosis or treat an ailment. We come out much the worse for wear. So, we deal in preventive medicine and actual clinical care, which means vaccinations, routine parasite checks, diet evaluation, oral checkups, and exhibit evaluation [trying to make sure the exhibits are safe for the animals and their keepers]."

Detecting an injury or sign of illness—early enough to provide useful medical treatment—is a critical part of this preventive approach. Early detection, however, is also one of the most difficult challenges facing vets and keepers alike. The reason, of course, is that most animals in the wild are programmed not to reveal any sign of weakness, at the risk of

attracting predators or indicating vulnerability to rivals within their own group. This instinct carries over into captivity. A young monkey, for example, masked a broken arm whenever the keepers and vets—potential "predators"—came near him. Finally, he was caught with his guard down by a Zoo visitor, who reported the injury. Other animals have managed to camouflage painful broken teeth for weeks or even months, and there have been instances, said Meier, "when animals were riddled with cancer but we didn't even know they were sick until a couple of days before they died. When animals have a lot of hair, it's difficult to judge their actual body condition."

These are rare examples, however, of animals that have managed to slip through what is on the whole an extremely effective early-warning system. As keepers feed the animals under their care, clean their exhibits, and interact with them in little ways during the day, they constantly look for subtle changes in an animal's activity, food consumption, and behavior, since any such variations may indicate a disease or injury. Equally valuable is a keeper's ability to eye an animal and know, from having made daily observations, that it is losing weight or moving in a slightly different way and thus should be examined by a vet.

At the Wild Animal Park, as field keepers make their morning feed and inventory runs, they also survey all the species in their exhibit, making a sight evaluation of as many individual

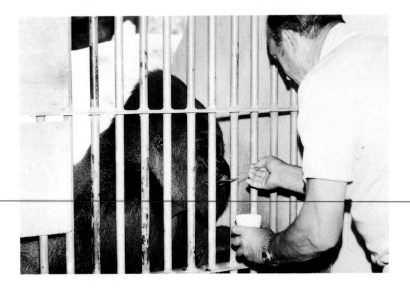

The lowland gorilla Trib has learned to take his vitamins from a spoon.

Zoo keepers routinely trim the elephants' overgrown toenails and overly thick foot pads.

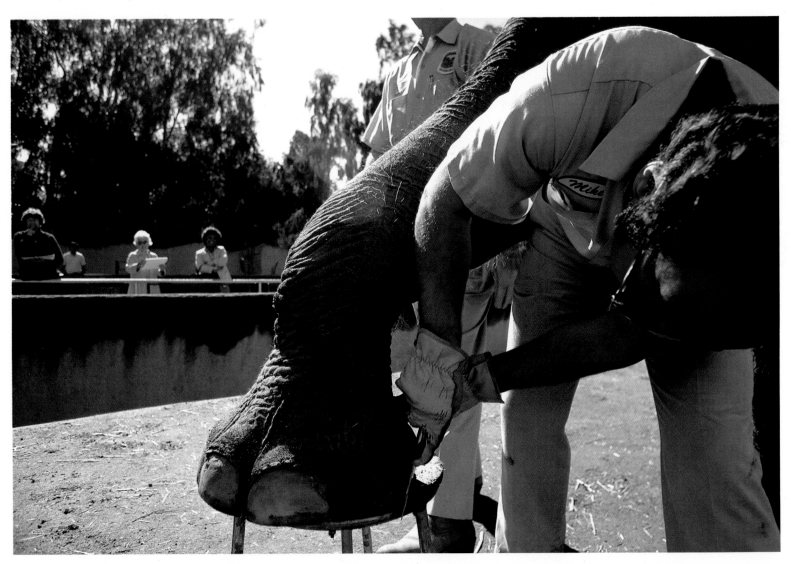

animals as possible. If necessary, binoculars are used to check for signs of diarrhea, limping, cuts or lacerations that might have occurred in a fight, developing pregnancies, or approaching births. "For the most part," said retired Park veterinarian Lester Nelson, "keepers are the key to what's going on out in the field. We only have two vets here, and it's impossible for us to get to each exhibit every day. What's more, we didn't see the animal in question yesterday, unless it's a particularly valuable animal that we're monitoring. The keepers know the animal's history and its particular habits [such as whether it is inclined to fight or not]. So, we rely on their trained judgments."

Since day-to-day observation of the animals is crucial, keepers maintain diaries of each field exhibit, noting any new or ongoing health or behavioral problems. These diaries, together with daily keeper reports, keep the curators and vets updated about developments out in the field. They also provide relief keepers with a good idea of what to expect in the exhibits they will be working in on a given day. The following excerpts from the Asian Plains diary of early 1982 are a representative sampling of the types of observations recorded:

January 3: The big male altai wapiti was very aggressive to Lasai at the hay feeder—gave Lasai a few good shots of antlers before Lasai moved away. No injuries (this time).

January 4: The male wapiti very aggressive again to Lasai. He ate almost the whole tub while Lasai stood by helplessly.

January 12: The nilgai male making his bid to become dominant, chasing WAP 46 fiercely, all over back of the exhibit. No contact or fighting observed.

A chisel, sledgehammer, crowbar, and quarter-inch electric drill were needed to extract a tooth from Lucky, an Asian elephant.

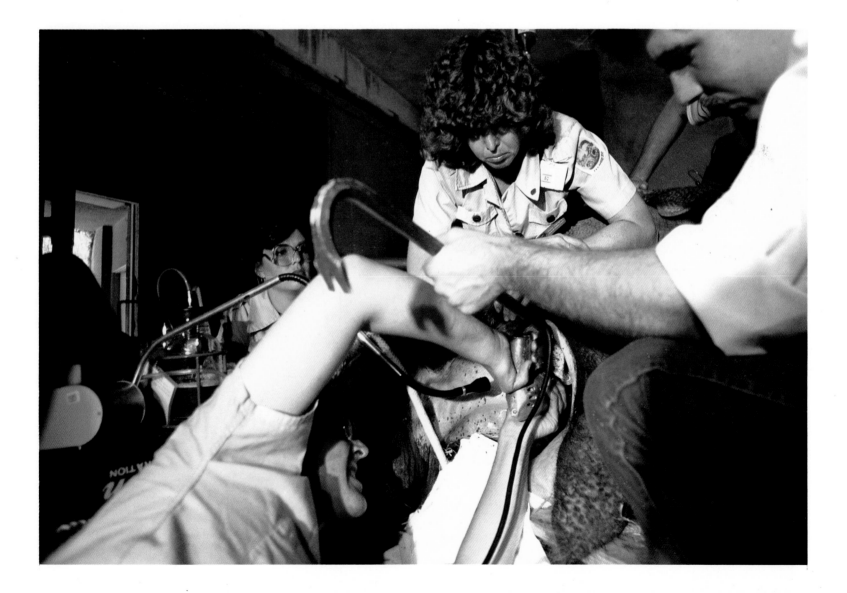

January 21: Everybody seems to be maintaining well despite the cold and rain.

January 23: Elburz red sheep: Several adult males, seven or eight, really going at it today, powerful ramming and lots of chasing. Sounded like firecrackers exploding. Very impressive.

February 5: Youngest male saiga spent most of morning harassing bachelor blackbuck. No injuries either side.

February 10: Both the two big wapiti males and two sambar males got into sparring matches this morning. No injuries occurred.

April 2: Persian gazelles: One female (WAP 19) favoring right front. She has an overgrown hoof on that extremity. Limp doesn't look serious.

April 5: Red Sheep: "Big Red" (WAP 01) is really starting to show his age; not much of a threat to keepers anymore.

April 9: Persian gazelles: Female (WAP 33) has a good-sized bag and is very close to dropping.

April 11: Big bellies and bags, but no babies.

April 17: Lasai very excited this afternoon. Came running up to dump truck, snorting and swinging his head. His behavior has been abnormally irritable and aggressive for several days. No indication that either female is stimulating him to act this way.

April 18: Blackbuck: Male (WAP 92) in the center still harassing the barasingha and anyone else who enters his new territory.

Always conscious of preventive medicine, the veterinarians try to examine the animals' teeth whenever possible for they know that, just as with humans, oral and dental care can greatly affect overall health. This was certainly true for Lucky, a forty-year-old Asian elephant at the Zoo, who had been steadily losing weight for nearly a year (an estimated 500 to 700 pounds), despite the fact that she had been consuming the same daily diet for years. Stool samples showed that Lucky wasn't digesting her food well, and the problem was traced to a molar—the size of a one-pound coffee can—that was out of alignment and thus causing her to get less food value from the same amount of hay. So Lucky was anesthetized and a chisel, a sledgehammer, a crowbar, and a quarter-inch electric drill were used to remove the offending molar.

Other exotic cases have arisen in recent years, providing vets with still greater knowledge of animal dentistry. Noted Jane Meier, "In the wild, predators, parasites, or disease kill most creatures before oral hygiene becomes a major health factor. However, captive animals live longer than their uncivilized counterparts, and some of the Zoo's animals might live even longer if we knew more about oral diseases and how they affect overall metabolism."

Since oral pathology is a contributing factor in a number of animal deaths at the Zoo each year, vets must deal with the problem from a clinical viewpoint: performing oral examinations and surgical procedures on a widely disparate, though uniformly recalcitrant, group of patients. "Fortunately," said Phil Robinson, "most oral disorders respond well to conventional dental therapy." For example, in 1977, when Linda, the pygmy chimpanzee, was pregnant she broke off a front tooth during a skirmish. The vets were particularly concerned because they feared that the broken tooth might abscess and thus result in a miscarriage. But thanks to prompt dental treatment, which included corrective gum surgery, the problem was corrected and a few months later Linda safely delivered her eighth offspring.

Once a disease or injury has been detected, the next problem becomes one of administering treatment. If, for example, an animal must receive antibiotics or medicine of any kind, how do you get it down its throat without risking your hand? Writing in ZOONOOZ, animal health technician Terry Willingham described the subterfuge that is often required at the Zoo hospital when trying to get the patients to take their daily medication. Generally, she noted, medication is put on or in a food that is irresistible to the animal, and it's up to the hospital keepers to determine just what that animal's particular gustatory weakness is. Maggie, for example, a Baird's tapir, would happily take her capsules as long as they were embedded in slices of banana. And young pygmy chimpanzees will readily drink their decongestants and antibiotics, even with the bitter taste, if it's mixed with soda pop and then followed by a chaser of straight pop. At the Park, when gorilla keeper Sue Kennedy must administer oral antibiotics in capsule form, she makes what she calls medicine sandwiches. "I break a capsule open and spread the powder on a piece of bread, then I cover it with honey or peanut butter and top it off with another piece of bread."

Keepers have also found food treats effective when working with certain endangered and dangerous animals, for, using the food as a lure, they can often get close enough to the animal to apply topical medication to lacerations, scrapes, or bruises.

Dr. David Fagan, the Zoo's former dentist, works on the gorilla Trib's teeth.

Keeper Sue Schafer uses hydrogen peroxide to treat a wound on the male Komodo monitor's jaw. She holds the broom as a precaution.

This was certainly true with Nicky, the Park's young black rhino, who had to be treated for a fungus that was growing on his chest. "We had to entice him like this for two weeks," said curator Larry Killmar, "but Nicky got to the point where he actually looked forward to the treatment; he'd come up to us and want to be sprayed with the medication because he loved to get his apples and his carrots. We normally don't encourage contact with people, but it worked out beautifully in this situation because otherwise we would have had to trap him in a boma and keep him there—in a stressful situation—until we completed the treatment."

When an animal requires an injection, however, gaining its cooperation is quite a different matter (especially when the injections must be given daily over a period of time). Generally, the animals must be placed in a "squeeze cage"—a large box or crate whose barred walls, floor, and ceiling can be pushed inward to confine an animal in an increasingly small space—so that injections (and medication) can be properly and safely administered.

In those situations when an animal has to be treated in its own enclosure, modern immobilizing drugs allow the veterinarians to work safely within the exhibit's bounds. "In the past," said keeper Ken Willingham, "when we wanted to trim hooves on our zebras, we had to restrain them with a rope while we worked. Now we can tranquilize them, which is risky, but not nearly as stressful on the animal or as dangerous to the people involved."

When injured or ailing Zoo animals have to be transported to the hospital for treatment, they are either immobilized on the grounds with a blowgun (occasionally a dart gun must be used) or herded into a shipping crate. At the Zoo the "darting" procedure is relatively safe and predictable, since the veterinarians can get close to the animals and then shoot from a stable position. But this is not the case at the Wild Animal Park (between 350 to 400 animals are immobilized here every year—for medical treatment as well as shipment) where just getting close enough to the target animal to make a safe shot can be a major problem. "One frustration," said former Park veterinarian Lester Nelson, "is that certain animals will stand and watch us approach in a truck, but scatter the moment we turn the motor off. So we have to let the truck idle and it jiggles as we try to aim at a very small target, perhaps right between the horns of an animal in the foreground. But we

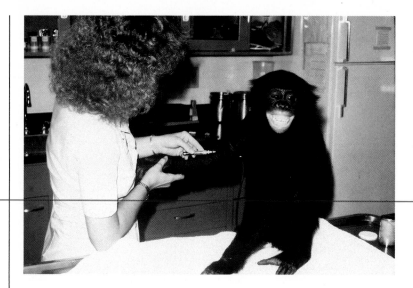

Animal health technician Terry Willingham administers an injection to a pygmy chimp, whose "smile" is actually a fear grimace.

Chico, the male African elephant at the Park, has a tumor removed from his trunk.

can't wait all day to get the 'perfect' shot. Sometimes an animal has been in a fight or has a broken leg and we absolutely have to get it out of there quickly for its own good."

In order to bring down hard-to-approach species, the vets must resort to a number of subterfuges. They often hide near feeding stations, climbing inside rock shelters that have been built to protect the trees from the animals. "This is fine," said Nelson, "until the rhinos come around and try to push the rocks aside with their horns to see what we're doing. We used to take wildebeests [gnus] from up in the trees [until they became suspicious] because they never thought to look up for 'predators' and they would come right past us." Once, when a half-dozen impala males had to be taken out for shipment, a different vehicle was used for each immobilization. "The impalas maintain a long 'flight distance' [the distance to which an animal will let danger approach before fleeing]," Nelson noted, "and when you take one shot from a truck, it's two weeks before you can get close to them again in that same truck. So we've used everything: a dump truck, the bucket of a skip loader, even the monorail as it passed by the herd."

Once an animal has been hit by an immobilizing dart, the problems for vets and keepers are often just beginning. Some animals stay put, calmly succumbing to the drug, but others start running around the exhibit until the drug finally takes effect, usually after about ten or twenty minutes. In either

case, since the drug renders the animal totally defenseless, keepers in several trucks are needed to try to keep it out of trouble and protect it from other animals. Even so, problems do occur. In 1981, for example, when the number two male in the sable antelope herd started to challenge the herd sire for supremacy, a situation developed which was hard to control. "They were squaring off and getting pretty aggressive," said Nelson, "but we didn't want the challenger to be the breeder, so we had to remove him for shipping. Once he was immobilized, however, he started running and prancing about—which he normally wouldn't do. The herd male doesn't tolerate that kind of behavior from other males and when he saw it, he attacked before we could get between them. They stirred up so much dust, we couldn't even see them, but apparently once the challenger fell down, the other male was satisfied and backed off. The challenger had a couple of gore wounds, but nothing serious, and once he recuperated we shipped him out."

Another danger comes when an immobilized animal heads instinctively for a pond in the exhibit, running into the water before a keeper can cut him off. Keepers often have to run right into the water to grab the animal and guide it to safety, but several animals have still been lost over the years. When an animal has been drugged, it loses control over its swallowing reflex, and if it submerges for only a few seconds, it can get water in its lungs and die. Nevertheless, immobilizing animals out in the field is a necessary risk that must be taken in order to provide for the overall well-being of a diverse animal population.

Risks are certainly involved whenever an animal must be anesthetized for surgery at either the Park or the Zoo hospitals. Yet, so many breakthroughs have been made in recent years—in terms of anesthesia techniques, the advent of new drugs, and the equipment used to administer them—that both hospital staffs routinely and safely perform operations that were once considered too much of a gamble. As recently as the 1960s, Jane Meier pointed out, incapacitating an animal for surgery was risky, for the patient would frequently go into shock and die. "Therefore, unless a problem was compelling and the animal's health in obvious jeopardy, most zoos were content to let well enough alone."

Even today, in working with such a wide array of patient species and sizes, considerable experimentation is often re-quired before an optimum drug dose can be ascertained. "We try to extrapolate from experience with domestic animals," said Meier, "and when we don't have that experience, we try the recommended dosage on a related, but less valuable, specimen." This is what the vets did before operating on the broken leg of a female Komodo monitor, who presumably incurred her injury by falling from an artificial rock in the exhibit area.

"The Komodo monitor breathes irregularly and can hold its breath for fifteen minutes or longer," said Jim Bacon, the general curator of reptiles. "That's unique right there. Plus, nobody had ever anesthetized one before. So, the vets first experimented on a water monitor—a close relative—and when this worked, they used a similar technique to repair the leg of the Komodo. During the sham operation [which caused no lasting harm to the water monitor], they opened her leg up and studied her muscles and circulatory vessels so they would also have an idea of what they were going to see when they opened up the Komodo." Added Jane Meier, "A generation ago, no one would have dared to try to remedy an injury like that. Either the leg would have mended itself or the reptile would have learned to function as best it could. But we were able to bend a stainless steel bone plate to approximate the conformation of the humerus and affix it to the bone with cortical bone screws. Later radiographs showed complete healing of the bone."

Another history-making repair job, this time on a somewhat larger but no less endangered species, came in 1980, when doctors at the Park used innovative surgical procedures to fix an elephant's broken leg.

In September of that year, the female African elephant Mandavu fractured her right rear leg when she fell into the moat surrounding the Park's elephant enclosure. Before that time, captive elephants were often euthanized after suffering a severe leg injury, and only a handful of elephants had ever been treated successfully for leg fractures such as this—all of them requiring bone-plating techniques that offered a limited possibility of success at best. When X rays revealed that Mandavu had a 3-1/2 inch overlap of broken portions of her tibia, and after consulting with vets at zoos around the country, Park officials decided that bone-pinning was the method most likely to succeed. "We ruled out everything else," said Lester Nelson.

Mandavu stands in her stall at the Park's elephant barn follow- ing a successful operation to re- pair her broken leg.

"The biggest minus factor was that this method hadn't been tried before on an elephant, but we couldn't see logically why it shouldn't work."

Thus, special casting material was flown in from San Francisco, a special one-inch-in-diameter stainless steel pin was developed to hold the healing bones in place, and surgical equipment was rounded up, including handsaws and power drills. Since the 7,000-pound Mandavu was certainly too heavy to transport to the hospital, Park vets had to move all the necessary equipment to the elephant barn. Mandavu's leg was X-rayed there and surgery took place on October 9, with veterinarians, physicians, orthopedic technologists, a machinist, and seven elephant keepers in attendance. "After we had her drugged, I absolutely didn't want the operation to last over six hours," said Nelson. "An elephant can wind up with pneumonia or a collapsed lung if you have her lying on her side longer than that."

Fortunately, surgery took less time than expected (under four hours) and afterwards Mandavu was outfitted with a special cast. When the cast was changed for the first time, four weeks after the operation, the leg was healing so well that the pin fell right out. Apparently, enough calcium had formed around the bone that the pin was no longer needed. After the third cast change, X rays showed almost complete calcification near the fracture—and this less than three months after the operation. Said Nelson, "Mandavu's regular diet [approxi-

mately 150 pounds of Sudan grass and oat hay each day, along with acacia browse and the special horse feed called omaline] supplied all the needed calcium and mineral requirements to allow a relatively speedy recovery." He also noted that had this injury occurred in the wild, Mandavu would not have survived. "She would not have been able to hobble more than 400 to 500 feet to get food or water."

Mandavu adjusted well to her injury and the cast, but not to the fact that she had to be kept in isolation in the barn (this was done in order to prevent the other elephants from pulling away the cast's supporting fiberglass wrap and thus possibly reinjuring the leg). Three months of isolation is not an easy adjustment for an animal like the elephant to make, especially since it forms close herd bonds. "She didn't eat very well and she wasn't very happy," noted keeper Torrey Pillsbury. But finally her leg was healed to the point where, even with a final cast still on, she was let out among her old friends in the main enclosure. They accepted her immediately (she didn't have to fight for her original spot within the herd's hierarchy) and they enjoyed playing with her cast, pulling off the gauze and throwing it above their heads. Meanwhile, Mandavu appeared to relish her regained freedom, hobbling around the pen and rubbing her cast on rocks, tree trunks, and concrete edges. Soon, she and the other elephants managed to remove the cast.

From its earliest years, the Zoological Society of San Diego has placed a high premium on the medical well-being of its resident animals, thus perpetuating the professional and personal concerns of founder Harry Wegeforth. One of the first zoo directors to hire a full-time veterinarian, Wegeforth also served as a consultant whenever needed. Drawing on his medical knowledge and his keen sense of animal behavior, he would often help treat the animals who were ailing, or suggest a method of treatment.

In 1926, with a $50,000 donation from Ellen Browning Scripps, Wegeforth built the Zoo's first hospital, one of the only zoo hospitals in the world at the time. Alas, the building itself was somewhat lacking, with absolutely no running water and no heat in the high-ceilinged rooms upstairs. In addition, in order to earn $5,000 annually from the county, Wegeforth converted the more desirable ground floor spaces, renting them out to the State Poultry Diagnostic Laboratory. Here, the Zoo's second veterinarian, John Whiting, spent most of his

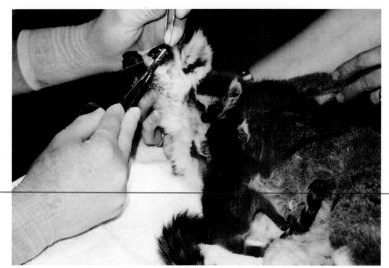

A ring-tailed lemur's lacerated eye is sutured in the company of her offspring, after it was decided that being present at the operation would be less traumatic for the babies than being separated from their mother.

Corrective surgery was required when this fast-growing emu, named Herkimer, developed progressively worse twisting of the tibiotarsal (drumstick) bone. Complications at the fracture site necessitated a lightweight body cast for a month, and a conventional baby-walker, padded with pillows, kept Herkimer off his feet for about two weeks as part of his postoperative care.

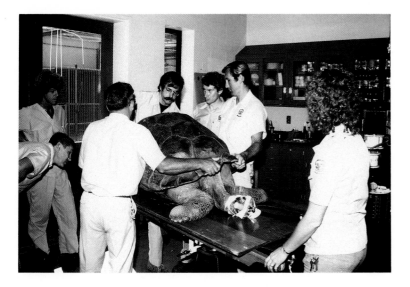

Zoo veterinarians remove a tumor from a Galápagos tortoise.

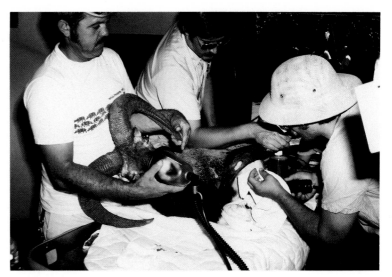

A mouflon, gored earlier in the day by a Nilgiri tahr, is treated at the Park hospital.

time examining an endless stream of chickens and turkeys for *salmonella pullorum*, coccidiosis, blackhead, and other diseases affecting poultry. But despite these admittedly poor working conditions, Wegeforth still managed to recruit some excellent medical talent and they busily set to work upstairs.

In the mid-1970s, concerned that the original hospital had become too small to accommodate the Zoo's ever-burgeoning activities, Joe Jennings became the principal benefactor for the modern medical center that bears his name. Opened in 1977, this two-story building is adjacent to the original Zoo hospital (which now houses the Research Department). One of Jennings's particular concerns was that the Zoo be able to provide sophisticated health care for the increasing number of endangered species on its grounds. As a result, the new hospital features an elaborate surgical amphitheater with a large and versatile hydraulic operating table that can accommodate nearly all species. Also, the recovery room is padded on all sides, including the floor, and this minimizes the possibility that an animal will injure itself when, in a disoriented state, it awakens from anesthesia.

Another ongoing project at the hospital has been to gather data on the various medical problems afflicting animals at the Zoo and the Wild Animal Park. Veterinary virologists are now studying viral diseases common to exotic animals while two pathologists are investigating the causes of animal deaths. It is hoped that their findings will not only prevent the spread of disease and parasites among the Society's own wildlife collection, but will contribute to life-saving efforts at other zoological institutions as well.

When animals die at the Zoo and the Park—which happens throughout the year from disease, broken bones, conflicts with other animals, and plain old age—the Society learns from the disappointments, since each animal is subject to a mandatory necropsy. The veterinary staff are thus able to draw on detailed records, examining the various causes of death in past years, and this in turn can lead to better medical care for the animals presently in the collection.

This knowledge, however, does not really ease the sadness felt by curators, keepers, and veterinarians when a favorite animal dies. "We're not always dealing with nameless faces," noted Phil Robinson. "Certain animals become very well known to the public and when they become ill, it's a matter of concern to quite a few people." Keepers, especially, are encouraged not to grow overly attached to their animals, but they still suffer keen disappointment when they lose an animal that has been in their care for many years. Bob, the orangutan, was an immensely popular animal who, in his mid-twenties, began suffering from a chronic sinus condition. Vets and keepers spent many months trying to keep him healthy, including

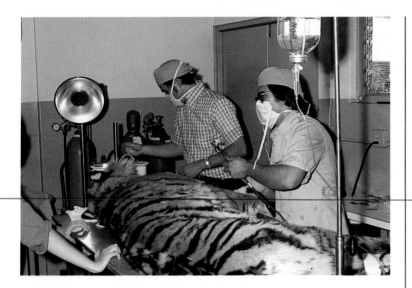

Cataracts are removed from a Siberian tiger.

Surgery is performed on a cheetah in the operating room of the Jennings Center, the Zoo's modern hospital facility.

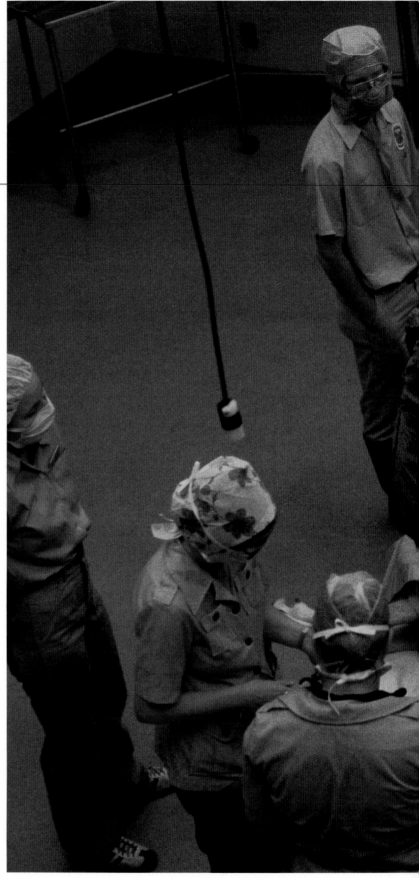

treatments that required over twenty anesthetic procedures, but finally he began to refuse his food. "He died while we were working on him," recalled keeper Ken Willingham. "It was like losing a close friend."

Of course, there are also the day-to-day, week-to-week vigils that help pull an animal through a medical crisis. As Willingham noted, "I remember an old keeper, Roger Temple, who worked with the gorillas. One of his favorites was a young male, Junior, who became seriously ill at one time. In fact, the vets in charge of health care at that time had given up hope and felt they should put Junior to sleep, but Roger said, 'Let's give him a last chance.' Roger hand-fed him at the hospital and nursed him back to health. When Junior returned to the other gorillas, Roger would put a little red sweater on him when it was cold, and every morning he would come down to the cage, pull up his green stool, then sit down with a cup of coffee and say, 'Well, Junior, how are you doing today?'" Junior now lives in Kansas City (where he is known as Big Mac), and he is a very healthy gorilla.

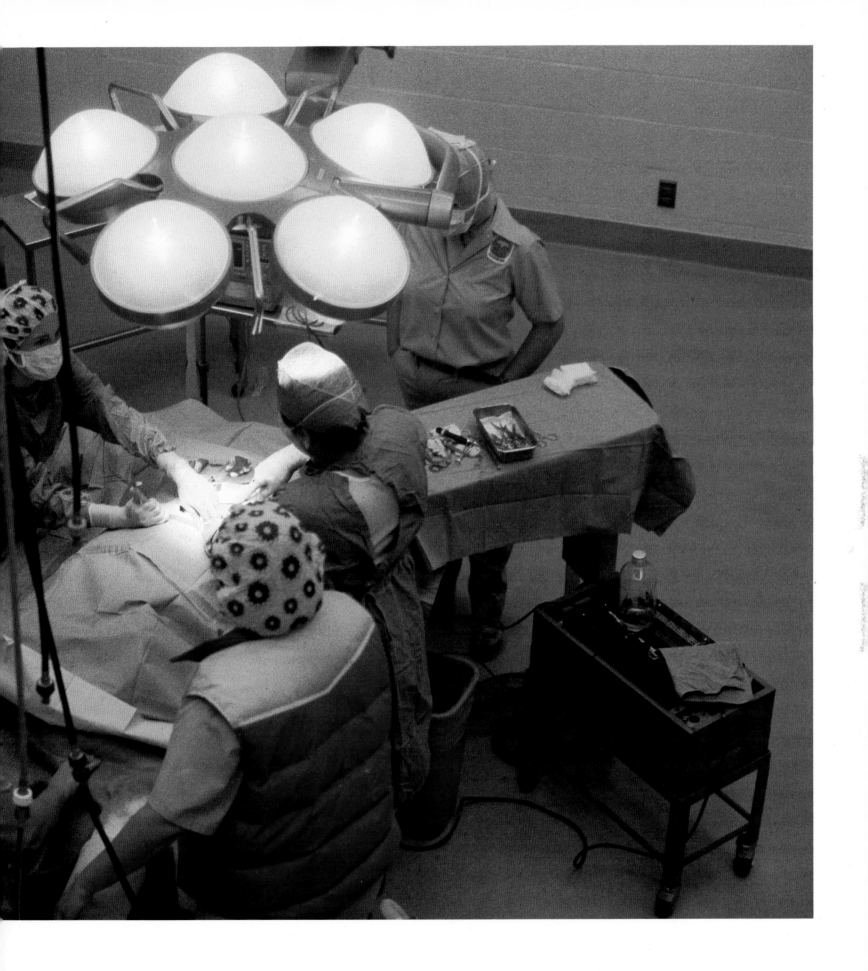

ANIMAL MANAGEMENT AT THE PARK

When John Fairfield arrived as the Wild Animal Park's first head keeper in 1970, two years before it opened to the public, he admittedly had no real training for the adventure that lay ahead. "I had over twenty years of experience in *zoo* zoos," he pointed out, "but the Park was a completely innovative concept, and none of us involved really knew the way it was going to work. I had a few answers, but not nearly as many as were needed. So, we just worked our tails off and hoped for the best."

Two of Fairfield's earliest employees were keepers Carmi Penny and Larry Killmar, both of whom had been working at the Zoo. Once he had trained them in the rudiments of the job, they in turn helped break in other new keepers. "Most of the animals were kept in large holding pens until the main field exhibits were completed," Fairfield recalled, "but keep in mind that while we were trying to train all our keepers from scratch, handle the incoming animals, and move animals around, the construction crews were laying the monorail bed. There were bulldozers, surveyors, engineers, and dynamite crews all over the place. We also had animals that were flighty, highly nervous, and hard to work with under the best of con-

ditions. Then somebody would set off ammonium nitrate and blow half the side of a hill away. . . . Well, it was enough to put a strain on a guy."

Once the animals began to move into completed exhibits, new challenges arose in terms of animal management. "Like how do you feed a 65-pound springbok and a 5,000-pound rhinoceros in the same enclosure?" asked Fairfield. "Well, by establishing separate feeders." Another early problem was that while the perimeter fencing kept the Park's animals from escaping, predators such as coyotes were frequently able to dig their way in, making off with the young babies of such species as the addra gazelle. The problem was somewhat alleviated when chicken wire was installed underneath the fencing.

Meanwhile, Jim Dolan, the curator in charge of animal acquisitions, was busy determining the population mix to go inside the five main field exhibits (North Africa, East Africa, South Africa, Asian Plains, and Asian Swamp). His decisions were based primarily on the geographic region the animals came from in the wild and on his own educated guess as to which species might peacefully coexist. One unsuccessful experiment involved the Grevy's zebras, who started out in the East Africa exhibit but eventually had to be moved to their

The gracefully built Thomson's gazelle is the most common type of gazelle found in Africa.

own hillside exhibit because they continually attacked young animals, especially baby wildebeests and springbok. "When a herd of zebras attack another animal, its chances are not very good," noted Carmi Penny. "We feel the problem could have been avoided had the exhibit been larger, but that wasn't possible." A similar trial effort was made with a Masai giraffe, who was placed in the South Africa exhibit. Typically curious and certainly nonthreatening, the giraffe was investigating the southern white rhinos the first day he was released when one rhino suddenly charged and fatally gored him in the chest.

As the Park's animal collection grew, and individual herds expanded to upwards of ninety to a hundred animals, several less aggressive species (such as the nyala, the slender-horned gazelle, and the Thomson's gazelle) began to fare poorly amidst the increasing competition and activity. For example, when the original groups of animals were smaller, the topi—an antelope that is extremely difficult to maintain and propagate in zoos—could go wherever they wanted to without getting into trouble. Eventually, however, the competition proved too severe and the existing animals had to be sent to the Zoo. Here's where the Zoological Society of San Diego benefited once again from the flexibility afforded by its two locations. "We didn't have to ship the topi to another zoo," said Larry Killmar, "or hope that they could somehow recoup out here."

The continuing population growth at the Park has made it necessary for keepers and curators not only to monitor the effects that overcrowding might be having on an entire exhibit, but to anticipate when this could produce a problem within a particular species. "In those species where we're having good success," said Killmar, "we try to determine the number of individuals we should keep—particularly males—in order to minimize conflicts and promote continued reproduction. We defeat the whole purpose out here if suddenly there are too many males in a herd and they spend so much time fighting and interacting that they forget about the females, and breeding ceases."

Just as the absence of a social group has proved to be a major deterrence to the white rhino's willingness to breed in captivity, so, too, overcrowding has been an inhibiting influence on the breeding habits of certain other species. Animals seem to have a physiological mechanism that responds to the stress of overpopulation, and it comes out when the males begin to compete continually with each other and the females miss their estrous cycles. This change in a herd's behavior was illustrated by the Persian gazelles, whose numbers had reached fifty-two at the beginning of 1982. "In their earlier years at the Park," said Carmi Penny, "most of the females gave birth twice a year. But as the group's numbers increased, and the population within the other species also grew, nearly all the females dropped to a single major calving season."

Fortunately, as Penny pointed out, a surplus of males within a group can sometimes have a positive effect on overall reproduction. "At one point, our white-bearded wildebeest population increased to where we had up to twelve adult males. Since they're highly territorial, this led to a lot of fighting, but in a year or two we began noticing that the overall herd was actually healthier with more males around. Where normally we could expect three or four babies to die out of a season's crop, our mortality rate dropped to practically zero and the babies appeared to be stronger." This success was probably the result of natural selection, where, just as in the wild, the two or three toughest, strongest males were breeding the females—thus passing their genes on to their offspring.

Like a veteran remembering his war stories, keeper Gerry Bender can clearly recall the day when a southern white rhino walked from his regular turf out through shallow water to an island in the South Africa exhibit. "We didn't want rhinos out on the island," said Bender, "because they ate the trees and other vegetation. So, about six or seven of us went out there to chase him off. We waved our arms and yelled, which usually makes the rhinos move away, but he spooked. He was on this little piece of land and he didn't know where to go, so he just took off—in my direction. I turned and ran to get out of his way, but when I looked back, he was still behind me. Finally, I just dove to the side and he ran past me, into the water." Although the rhino did step on Bender's foot, laying him up for several days, Bender was lucky to have escaped without more serious injury.

Fortunately, a field keeper's life at the Park rarely includes such explosive encounters with the animals in his or her care. "There have been a number of close calls out here," said Larry Killmar, "but in our first twelve or thirteen years—knock on wood—nobody has been seriously injured by an animal." Still, since keepers are in constant contact with the animals—filling feeders, cleaning up, taking daily animal inventory, processing

White-bearded wildebeests have been referred to as "the old fools of the veldt," because of their curious appearance.

newborn babies, aiding vets on immobilizations, and tending to exhibit repairs and improvements—the potential for danger is always there. "We don't really consider keepers trained until they've worked here for about two years," said Killmar. "There's too much to learn about what goes on out in the field for keepers to work safely and effectively with the animals before then. Even after that, a keeper can never think, 'Oh yeah, that's going to happen.' You can try to predict animal behavior and, with experience, you'll be reasonably accurate, but you never know what might fire an animal off."

As keepers gain insight into exotic animal behavior (which is not always the same in captivity as it would be in the wild), they learn to pick up the little signals that a particular animal will give off when it's in an aggressive mood. If the animal appears to have harmful intentions as they work nearby, they can usually read the signs and quickly retreat to the safety of a nearby truck should the need arise.

The Park once had an elu (the hybrid offspring of an eland and a kudu), who had horns that were about 2-1/2 feet long and a nasty, unpredictable temperament. "One day, he tipped over the cement drinker in his holding pen," keeper Rich Massena recalled, "so I went in with another keeper to fix it up. Well, I just looked in this animal's eyes and something told me that he was in one of his bad moods. I told the other keeper, 'Let's get out of here right now,' and we broke for the gate, but I didn't quite make it." The elu hit Massena just before he reached the gate, pinning him against the chain link fence. He was thus trapped between the elu's horns, but when the animal backed up to charge again, Massena saw his opening and quickly leaped to safety.

"Actually," said Carmi Penny when he was still working at the Park, "most of the animals out here want nothing to do with us as long as we provide their food. They tend to maintain a healthy 'flight distance.' But there are exceptions. The dominant male waterbuck weighs about 600 pounds and he would try to kill us if he had the opportunity. He's an extremely tough critter and we can never let our guard down when we're working in his exhibit. We once had a waterbuck who even fought with the rhinos, all the time, until he was fatally gored." Then there are the ostriches, especially the adult males, who are protective of their territory and extremely aggressive during their breeding season. They chase people and other animals, and readily attack keeper trucks—kicking in

The Cape buffalo is a stout-limbed animal with massive horns that join at the base. Although not yet endangered in the wild, it is a popular trophy animal sought by big-game hunters.

Blackbucks have long, curved corkscrew horns, but surprisingly few injuries occur when they fight. Here, two bachelor males engage in a ritualized challenge in order to hone their sparring skills should they ever decide to challenge an older male's territory.

front grills (before brush guards were installed to deter this), smashing in hoods (after jumping up on the trucks), shattering windshields, and knocking off side mirrors with well-aimed kicks.

Of course, other species at the Park hardly reflect the fearsome reputation they've earned elsewhere. Cape buffalo, for example, have attacked farmers and hunters in Africa and have gored keepers and veterinarians at other zoos. "This casts a bad light on the Capes we have here," said one Park keeper. "We can work around them because their attitude is pretty much, 'I'm not going to bother you, so don't bother me.' They even walk up to the feeders and want to be scratched with a rake."

Over the years, the population mix in the five field exhibits has been remarkably successful, as evidenced by the reproductive success of most of the species and the ability of nearly all of them to coexist peacefully. Yet since new species and new animals are continually being introduced into the overall collection—and since young animals born at the Park can grow into unruly adults—field keepers must constantly monitor animal interactions, interpreting and anticipating aggressive behavior that might disrupt the harmony of the whole. One blatant example of this kind of agitative behavior occurred when a group of Nilgiri tahr were introduced to the Asian

An ellipsen waterbuck prods a southern white rhino. This brazen behavior eventually back- fired when the waterbuck was fatally gored by a rhino.

A white-bearded wildebeest and a fringe-eared oryx sparring in 1969, soon after the Park began receiving animals.

Protective metal caps had to be placed on the tips of this Nilgiri tahr's horns to keep him from goring other species.

Swamp exhibit in 1979, and the adult male proceeded to gore two fallow deer and a mouflon. A strategy meeting was held and a solution first used by domestic dairy farmers was successfully adapted; the tips of the tahr's horns were trimmed and then flat metal caps were screwed onto the tops of them.

A less manageable situation has arisen between the dominant males in the waterbuck herd and the group of white-tailed wildebeests. "This has always been a problem out here, even when we switch males around," said Larry Killmar. "We try to alleviate conflicts like this because when animals of a different species fight each other, they have different types of horns or antlers and, when they come together, they can injure one another quite easily. For example, the wildebeest's horn will come down on either side of the waterbuck's eyes, and when the white-tail moves his head back and forth, the points of his horns rub right in the corners of the waterbuck's eyes." One waterbuck lost an eye fighting like this and, in a second altercation, lost his other eye—at which point his rival (the white-tailed wildebeest) took direct advantage of the situation and finished him off before the keepers could safely intervene. "This kind of fight to the finish is very uncommon out here," Killmar noted, "but these particular males did not get along

Baseballs were put on the horns of this overly aggressive Russian saiga to protect his neighbors in the Asian Plains exhibit. The remarkable feature of the saiga is its bulbous snout, which scientists feel may be an adaptation used for warming and moistening inhaled air in its native Siberian habitat.

with each other and the result is something that would have happened in the wild." Later, when another waterbuck male had to be isolated in a boma while his injured eye mended, Killmar hoped that he had learned his lesson about fighting with the wildebeests. Indeed, when the waterbuck returned to the field, he moved his herd away from the wildebeests to another area of the exhibit, and he tended to retreat from the direct challenges of his rival male. "The potential problems will continue as long as we have these two species together," said Killmar, "but we have no other choice. Both animals are too valuable to simply get rid of one, and we don't have an-

other exhibit that would suit either species, so we hope they can learn to live together."

While sometimes having to intercede to keep the peace, keepers are also able to enjoy some amusing interactions between species. "In the East Africa exhibit," said keeper Rick Barongi, "the giraffes want nothing to do with the pygmy hippos; they apparently are leery of an animal that looks so sinister and spends most of the day in the water. Yet I've seen a meek little sitatunga come over to where a hippo is eating, and the hippo will walk away. There's also a slender-horned gazelle in the exhibit who weighs less than 50 pounds but is

The most conspicuous feature of the ellipsen waterbuck, a water-loving antelope, is the white, elliptical ring that appears on its rump.

Although vast herds of white-tailed wildebeests once roamed the open plains of southern Africa, these animals are now extinct in the wild, surviving only on private farms, and in parks, game reserves, and zoos. Fortunately, the species breeds well in captivity and its future thus seems assured.

certainly not afraid of a 400-pound hippo. We call him Spud, and he's such an aggressive character—always charging the gardeners and the construction people—that we had to blunt his horns. One day, I filled a feeder down near the lakeshore and a hippo came up to get some of the alfalfa. Spud came over, took one look at the hippo—then charged him! The hippo stood his ground, opened his mouth, and snapped away, and I thought, 'Spud is a goner.' But he was so quick, he was able to hit the hippo up on the roof of his mouth with his horns before the hippo could chomp down.''

When a male dromedary camel (who was being used for the rides in Nairobi Village) had to be separated from his two female companions during his rut, the North Africa exhibit was selected as his temporary home. This exhibit features an impressive herd of addax, and keepers feared that the females might gore the poor camel if he innocently walked up to a mother and her baby. "The addax are the most protective, aggressive mothers out here," said keeper Randy Rieches. "They're not afraid of us and they even attack our trucks when we try to get near, so we felt they certainly wouldn't be scared of the camel. And since they have babies throughout the year, we knew we had to really keep a close eye out when he was introduced." Well, while keepers were poised to come to the camel's rescue, the addax—as well as the addra gazelles—fled to the very back of the exhibit at the first sight of this strange, one-humped creature. They had never seen a camel before, and

they stayed well away for the next two days, not even coming down at night to eat from their feeders. Finally, they worked up enough courage—and hunger—to risk going near to the camel, but not without closely watching his every move.

Most of the species who live in the Park's field exhibits have enough animals to form dominance hierarchies, where each individual knows its ranking within the group. Normally, a dominant herd male stays with all the females and the young, while the adolescent males are driven out to join a bachelor herd that consists of other older males as well. This helps the females when they have newborns, for it eliminates the confusion that adolescents generate when they are still in the main herd. Also, it's safer for the calves when the bachelor males have been forced to the periphery and are not competing and running around within the main herd.

Because it limits competition, and thus reduces potentially fatal injuries to valuable and endangered animals, a rigid dominance hierarchy is especially welcomed in a captive setting like that which exists at the Wild Animal Park. The older males still compete, but the winners who take over a territory generally maintain it without having to face repeated challenges. The animals within a herd remain familiar with one another because they can't wander out, nor can newcomers wander in; this is unlike the wild where herd males must constantly prove themselves anew. "Once two animals meet and they

This solitary dromedary camel caused quite a stir when he was introduced to the North Africa exhibit, but the addax and addra gazelles eventually learned to accept his presence.

A blackbuck, or sasin antelope, presides over his harem. The Park's prolific blackbuck herd totals nearly one hundred, with about ten males maintaining territories of varying size. Each male has scent glands underneath his eyes, which he uses to mark off his territory. He tries to entice as many females as possible to join him, but will fight any male who attempts to enter his domain.

decide—through a fight or simple intimidation—who is going to be above the other, it will normally stay that way until the dominant male grows too old," explained keeper Barongi. "Here at the Park, the younger males learn to respect the herd male, and when they do grow big enough to oppose him, they may avoid that challenge simply because he has the psychological edge."

Of course, some potentially nasty skirmishes are avoided by purposely shipping the young challengers out before they have had a chance to overthrow the herd male. This is done especially in those cases where the existing herd male is a proven breeder, is still in his prime, and is part of an endangered species. Keepers let the prolific species such as blackbuck and axis deer work out their territorial disputes without any interference, but they use "preventive management" with the rarer animals. "We'll take some males out as soon as they reach a certain age, *before* we see any aggression," Barongi explained, "because we know a particular exhibit is too small and ultimately the younger male would get killed by the older male." This is especially true in the smaller off-exhibit enclosures that contain slender-horned gazelles, Grevy's zebras, and Przewalski's horses. But the philosophy also applied to the Indian rhinos in the Asian Plains exhibit, where keepers stepped in and removed Lasai's son, Pandu, just before his third birthday. Lasai was beginning to chase Pandu, who thought this was a game. But the two were heading for a serious confrontation and Pandu stood to get badly hurt. There simply wasn't enough room in the exhibit to afford him a place to escape to.

Occasionally, the conflict between animals will take place later in the day, after the keeper trucks have left, or during the night. Thus, as soon as the keepers enter their exhibits in the morning, they look around to see if any animals are in trouble. One morning, the keepers in the East Africa exhibit spotted a male ostrich stuck in the mud at the edge of a pond that was being drained. The breeding season was approaching and apparently the older male ostrich in the group had chased his rival out into the pond. Four or five keepers had to handle the rescue, tying ropes around the ostrich's body and then pulling him in to shore.

Some animals have been reluctant to show their "appreciation" for similar rescue attempts. When a newly introduced female black rhino was chased into the water by the male, a half-dozen keepers had to go out to keep her from drowning.

An addra gazelle calf "hides" from potential predators. This behavioral pattern poses a challenge for keepers assigned to inventory the number of animals in each exhibit.

But once they had guided her back to shallow water and she had made her way safely onto shore, she turned around and wouldn't let the keepers come in. (The male had been chased away.) "Every time they tried to come out of the water, she threatened them," remembered former veterinarian Lester Nelson, "and she was big enough at the time that they didn't want to try calling her bluff. So, they had to wait out there in waist-deep water until another keeper drove her off with a truck."

When keepers "feed out" their exhibit in the morning, one of their responsibilities is to count all the animals and to look for those who are sick, injured, or newborn. This daily inventory is an important part of overall animal management at the Park because, through it, keepers gain a greater familiarity with each species and thus the ability to anticipate and assess animal behavior. "By seeing their animals out in the field day after day after day," said Carmi Penny, "keepers build up a memory of what is normal in a group and can thus sense an individual problem by noticing there's something out of character with the group as a whole. Keepers learn where the animals can be expected to be at different times during the morning and early afternoon and what their general behavioral patterns are, as a group and as individuals. This daily scrutiny makes it much easier to pick out problems than if we only concentrated on an inventory once a week."

Taking an accurate head count is a more difficult and time-consuming task when there are "hiders" among the exhibit's newborns. "Hiders" are either tucked away by their mothers in a protected place, such as an erosion ditch or between rocks, or will hide themselves as part of their innate anti-predator behavior. Most mothers tuck their babies in a new location every day, and keepers must find them, since a sick or injured baby can be saved if it is hand-raised at the Animal Care Center.

Every exhibit has rough terrain, where erosion has created innumerable hiding places, but keepers learn to know a mother's "tucking" patterns from one baby to the next, sometimes plotting this information on a map. This is especially useful when looking for Persian gazelles and Chinese water deer, for both species weigh only two to three pounds at birth and have been found inside spaces as small as a squirrel hole. It is also helpful in finding addra gazelles, since eight or ten babies may be hiding at any given time during the calving season. Occasionally, keepers are able to find babies by using mimic vocalization—either by vocalizing like a calf, which can cause a nervous mother to reveal where her calf is hiding, or by mimicking the mother, thus drawing the calf itself out of hiding. However, with a species like the red lechwe (an antelope), the more a keeper vocalizes, the farther away the mother will go.

By knowing an approximate birthdate for all pregnant animals—and through daily visual clues such as expanding milk sacs—keepers can better anticipate when to search for a new baby, especially if the expectant mother is apt to leave her babies unattended in a highly camouflaged spot.

"If one crew is unable to find a particular baby, or an expectant mother who is adept at hiding," said Larry Killmar, "we will bring in another crew and comb the entire exhibit area." One morning, keepers were searching the Asian Swamp exhibit for a pregnant Eld's deer who was due to give birth any day. Killmar joined the hunt, commenting, "With this particular female there's no real concern about her being a good mother, but we'd like to know if she gave birth overnight. This is an endangered species and they're so valuable we don't want to lose a baby."

Yet another responsibility of the field keepers involves the initial care they must give all newborns. When a mother is not aggressive toward keepers, this processing is a relatively easy task. The baby's umbilicus is soaked with a six percent solution of iodine and water to help protect the baby from neonatal diseases and infection when it lies down in mud or dirt. The animal is then weighed, measured, and inoculated against infancy diseases and viruses. By handling the baby, keepers are also able to look for any physical problems, such as blindness or leg injury, that might necessitate hand-raising. Finally, the baby's ear is notched and an identification number is tattooed on it. This enables keepers and vets to identify accurately animals out in the field from several hundred yards away, using binoculars. It also enables the Park personnel to maintain detailed records, including breeding records and relative growth studies, for each animal. "In the beginning our identification process was antiquated, to say the least," Killmar admitted. "We were guessing many times, and you can't be effective managing a collection this large by having guesswork be a part of identification. So, we started a notching and tattooing system that has been extremely successful."

All this may sound straightforward enough, but when certain species are involved—notably the addax and the white-bearded wildebeest—the tagging procedure can be difficult and dangerous, thus requiring quick action and teamwork.

The addax mothers, as noted earlier, are fiercely protective of their young. "They're consistently one of the most dangerous animals we have to contend with because they're not intimidated by us whatsoever and they have long corkscrew horns," said Killmar. "Mothers with a baby often charge the keeper trucks, occasionally putting holes in the sides. Even an aggressive mother whose nearby calf is not involved in a particular tagging will try to attack us because she feels threatened by our presence." This same challenge is posed by the wildebeest. "With most other animals, the mom runs away when keepers drive up and they can take five or ten minutes with the baby before turning it loose. But the wildebeest mom stays close to her baby and the keepers can't even jump out of the truck or she'll try to nail them. So they have to drive up, put a hoisting loop around the baby's neck, and pull it safely up into the truck for processing. Then they give it back to mom. They do the same thing with the addax."

Speed and timing are critical if keepers hope to process impala and wildebeest newborns—and avoid the need for hand-raising. These babies are "followers," as opposed to "hiders," and if keepers fail to reach them within five minutes of birth they will be up on their feet, running with their mothers. "We can chase after them with a truck and catch the baby,"

This sequence shows two Park keepers, Randy Rieches and Nancy Crowe, capturing a newborn blackbuck, ear-tagging the baby for identification purposes, and then releasing the baby back to its mother.

Two adult addax and a calf. Addax mothers are extremely protective of their young and will use their long corkscrew horns to try to prevent keepers from handling their newborns.

Axis deer, native to India and still secure throughout that country, are among the most prolific species at the Park.

said keeper Barongi, "but very often mom runs away—breaking the maternal bond—and it's also very stressful on the animals, so we avoid doing this."

In order to bypass some of these problems, the keepers post an early-morning watch (the time of day when most animals give birth) whenever they suspect that an impala or wildebeest is about to deliver. Once the calf drops, they give the mother several minutes to clean it off and to begin establishing a relationship with the calf (the "imprinting" process). Then, the keepers come up in a truck before the baby is able to run away. Their concern now is to avoid having the baby imprint on them instead of its mother, since this would mean that it would have to be hand-raised. Said Killmar, "In most cases, if you spend more than forty-five seconds with the baby wildebeest or impala, you run the risk of breaking the imprinting process. So, our keepers have learned to notch the baby's ears, determine its sex, and give it back to mom within forty-five seconds of capture."

The necessity of hand-raising a particular newborn animal can arise in several ways, and the decision is not always an easy one to make, for as one keeper noted, "The most exciting thing out here is to see a baby running with its mother." Still, certain situations are cut-and-dried, such as when keepers take too long notching certain babies and the mother then rejects the baby when it's released—refusing to nurse it—or the baby imprints on one of the keepers or even the truck and thus refuses to go to its real mother. This rarely happens, however. More often, the keepers determine that a newborn is too weak to survive out in the field, or that the mother does not appear

250

Opposite:
A Uganda giraffe grooms her calf inside a protective boma at the Park.

The powerfully built roan antelope is the third-largest of the antelope species after the eland and the kudu.

capable of maintaining it (or has been neglecting it for several days). When this happens, the baby is raised at the Animal Care Center until it is old enough to be either returned to a field exhibit or shipped to another zoo. Then, there's the fact that several herds at the Park have become so populous and are so prolific (the blackbuck and the axis deer, for example) that most of the babies are brought in for hand-raising, since they will eventually be shipped out anyway. It's much easier, and less stressful on the animals, to crate them up at the Care Center than to use a tranquilizing gun out in the field.

"We all feel it's desirable to let mothers raise their own babies," said Killmar, "but through experience and finding out the hard way, we know there are certain situations where we must automatically pull a baby for hand-raising. If we're dealing with something like a waterbuck, an impala, or an addra gazelle—and it's a cold, rainy day—then we're going to bring the baby into the Care Center without any hesitation. Who's to judge that a newborn should be brought in only if it's *absolutely* necessary? If we decide to wait another day, and then we find the baby dead, I think that's an unwarranted gamble to take with certain of our rare animals."

When keeper Rick Barongi first came to work at the Park, he admittedly hated to have to pull an animal for hand-raising. "I thought it would have too many problems when it was reintroduced into the herd. If it was a female, especially, I'd think, 'This animal is never going to let a male breed her, and if she does, she'll make a lousy mother and we'll have to hand-raise all her babies.' " Yet, he found that nearly all the females at the Animal Care Center who are released back into the field eventually produce offspring and take good care of them. "That kind of shocked me and I didn't believe it until I saw it for myself. Occasionally, the first baby born has to be hand-raised, but then natural instincts seem to take over. These animals also have a chance to watch other females of their species giving birth and caring for their babies."

Elsie the eland is a prime example of how a hand-raised female acclimated to her species and to her role in life. She was a neglectful mother with her firstborn, leaving the baby behind as she continually wandered off to visit the nearest keeper truck. Before she gave birth a second time, she was placed inside a boma (a sheltered corral), where she proved she could indeed be an attentive mother. Since then, she has raised all of her offspring—from the beginning—out in the main East Africa exhibit.

Bomas in each main exhibit are proving to be successful way stations between the headaches associated with hand-raising and the many dangers existing to newborns in the exhibit itself. One recent example involved the roan antelope species, which had not fared well at the Park since arriving in 1972. The two adult females had produced babies nearly every year, but these were being lost in the early weeks as a result of maternal neglect, accidents, or aggression by other animals (especially the male roan and the black rhinos). In order to improve the survival rate of the roan offspring, the female who had proven herself to be a good mother was placed inside a boma when she was pregnant. She had her baby inside this small area and she took care of him there for about three months, until he was big enough to fare for himself and stay out of trouble in the main exhibit.

The Park has several golden eagles on loan from the federal government. They are used in educational programs and in the bird show.

The addra gazelle is the largest of all true gazelles, standing 35 to 43 inches at the shoulder and weighing up to 160 pounds.

Fortunately, a mother's anti-predator instincts will oftentimes suffice when mother nature must be allowed to run its course, without human interference. In 1981, the golden eagles who live near the Park began preying upon addra gazelle babies in the North Africa exhibit. Since these babies stay "tucked" away from their mothers for about three weeks, they are especially vulnerable to predators such as the eagle and the coyote. "The addra gazelle is a valuable animal [costing $3,000 apiece]," noted Larry Killmar, "but the eagle is also endangered, and we certainly couldn't start shooting golden eagles just to save our animals." As it turned out, the dilemma was resolved by the animals themselves. Late one afternoon, when a keeper was working in the exhibit, he saw an eagle swoop down, grab a calf from behind with its talons, and try to fly off. The calf was too heavy, however, and dropped from the eagle's grasp. The eagle flew off for another try, but this time the baby's mother came running over, and when the eagle swooped down, she was there to defend her calf. Every time the eagle attacked, the mother stood ground right over the baby, all hunched up and jumping around, until finally the eagle gave up.

Several weeks later, keeper Barongi was in the exhibit and he watched as an eagle flew past a hillside. "The addra moms quickly got up and stood around watching the eagle," he said. "They now knew about this threat, and it was going to be a lot harder for the eagles to make off with a baby. When you see behavior like that, you can't say animals automatically lose their wild instincts in a captive situation like the Park."

One of the two North American bald eagles that are kept on exhibit in a free-flight aviary at the Zoo

RESEARCH AND CAPTIVE-BREEDING EFFORTS

n the walls inside his office at the Wild Animal Park, general curator Jim Dolan has color photographs of several of his favorite animals: the saiga, a bulbous-nosed animal from Siberia ("I think they're great," he chuckled), the rare Mhorr gazelle, and the Arabian oryx and the Przewalski's horse—two endangered species that have thrived in San Diego's overall collection. Above his desk, Dolan also has what he calls his "passenger pigeon" collection of aging black-and-white photographs. One shows the quagga, an animal that has been extinct since 1880, when the last survivor died in the Amsterdam Zoo. A second photo shows the last surviving Schomburgk's deer, which was bludgeoned to death inside a Buddhist temple in Thailand, where it was supposedly being protected. Then there's a Syrian wild ass, which died out as a species about 1929 when the last survivor expired in the Tiergarten Schönbrunn in Vienna. And finally there's a picture of the Burchell's zebra, which had been considered extinct since 1910, until a group was recently discovered in the Transvaal, South Africa.

"It's aggravating to know that people simply killed these animals off until they were extinct, and that I'll never be able to see them," Dolan remarked. "Yet looking at these photos reminds me that the person who'll be sitting in my office fifty years from now will want to see the animals that we're desperately trying to save today. This is an intensely personal feeling, but if I never achieve another thing in my life, I have a sense of fulfillment knowing that potentially what I'm doing today will have a positive effect on tomorrow. I'm sure most people who work at this kind of job feel the same way."

Certainly that attitude is shared by Dr. Kurt Benirschke, the charismatic director of the Society's Research Department, whose twenty-five person staff works closely with curators and keepers. "When I look at the situation very carefully," said Benirschke, "the only hope I can see for hundreds of species is really through captive-breeding efforts. We have absolutely no control over the wild today; it's all downhill for the animals who live there. And it is highly unlikely that we will have any influence, in the long run, over the areas from which a majority of our zoo animals come, whether you're

Dr. Kurt Benirschke and his "Frozen Zoo"—vials of sperm, ovum, and skin tissue from dozens of endangered animals

talking about mammals, primates, birds, or reptiles. Therefore, since we can no longer count on getting wild-caught animals to replenish our stock and to provide fresh genetic bloodlines, we must do all we can—through research efforts—to help build self-sustaining populations of exotic animals that we can manage from one generation to another."

After over twenty years as a practicing doctor and a noted university professor in the fields of human pathology and reproductive medicine, Benirschke decided to focus his attention on the reproductive problems of exotic wildlife, and with this in mind he accepted his current position at the Zoo in early 1975. He was joining a zoological society that had stressed scientific objectives ever since the 1920s, when Harry Wegeforth built the Zoo's first hospital and created a research council. Yet, Benirschke felt the board of trustees should place even greater emphasis on research efforts that could improve captive-breeding results and minimize life-threatening diseases within the Society's collection. He arrived with three assistants, and the research endeavor now embraces scientists in such disciplines as genetics, endocrinology, pathology, microbiology, and animal behavioral science. This reflects Benirschke's belief that there is "one medicine," or, put differently, that the work in one discipline invariably overlaps with and has consequences for the work in other disciplines.

Ironically, while man systematically destroys the wilderness environments around him, his medical knowledge and his breakthroughs in research may offer a partial repayment of the debt owed to endangered species. Although Benirschke believes that Zoo professionals can at best have only a minuscule impact on the survival of animals in the wild, he feels that it is still possible—through highly sophisticated breeding programs, "frozen zoos," modern medical treatment, and enlightened animal management—to ensure the ultimate survival of all those species in zoos today. For the near future, however, he stresses the enormous need for a basic understanding of the reproductive physiology and the behavioral patterns of virtually every endangered species.

"We know so much about human reproduction, and so little about exotic animals," he lamented. "It's very easy to talk about artificial insemination, but the public has no idea how difficult it is to actually try to do this with a rhinoceros, a tiger, an elephant, or a pygmy chimp. You must first learn *how* to collect the semen from these different species [this is done through electroejaculation] and how to freeze it. Then, you must know exactly *where* to put the semen inside the female, in order to fashion special instrumentation with which to do so. And you have to know *when* the female is going to shed her egg so that you can inject the semen at the right time. This means you must know the animal's ovulatory cycle. Thus, we must basically start from scratch with each animal in each species, until we begin to accumulate baseline knowledge here and at other zoos in the coming years."

The hormones that govern a female's reproductive cycle can be easily isolated from an animal's blood and identified, but since hormone levels must be studied daily, drawing blood is far too impractical when the patient is an exotic animal. As Zoo endocrinologist Bill Lasley told *Discover* magazine: "You won't get a gorilla to stick out its arm and give you blood—even once in a while." Thus, when he began working at the Zoo in 1975, Lasley pioneered a technique whereby hormone levels could be determined through urine. By evaluating the daily urine samples that are collected by keepers, Lasley and his associates are now able to monitor the reproductive cycle of females without creating a stressful situation. In turn, this enables Zoo personnel to plot various breeding strategies and to determine the progress of a particular pregnancy.

As Lasley pointed out in ZOONOOZ, knowing the precise time of ovulation is invaluable when forming breeding pairs within a limited zoo population, for it maximizes the chances that a successful pregnancy can be arranged. He cited Georgette, "a capuchin monkey who was ostracized from her group and not allowed to mate. We collected urine samples that determined the frequency of her ovulations, which were indicated by sharp rises of urinary estrogen and luteinizing hormone. After two ovulations had been recorded, the third was predicted and a timed mating was arranged. In this case, conception occurred . . . [and] Georgette gave birth on Valentine's Day, as expected . . ."

Knowing a female's normal estrous cycle is equally critical when using artificial insemination and embryo transfers, two methods which are widely successful with domestic cattle. San Diego researchers hope to emulate these programs, but as Benirschke cautions, "The techniques involved are largely unperfected in zoos today because we simply do not have enough basic research available. The cattle people have done their research because this is a lucrative way to do business. There's no money in this with giraffes or pygmy chimps—at least not today."

This is a cause of major frustration at many zoos today, for it is known that artificial reproductive methods would most certainly boost the populations of endangered species. With this technique, for example, adult males and females with behavioral abnormalities or particular partner preferences could still be utilized for reproduction. If a particular female did not allow normal mating, researchers could then monitor her normal ovulatory cycle through urine samples, collect semen from a male (or draw on semen already in cold storage), and then transfer it to the female when her estrogen level was at its peak—taking into account all the procedural problems noted by Benirschke. Indeed, artificial insemination has already been responsible for the arrival of several pandas in Peking and a gorilla in Memphis.

Artificial breeding methods would also allow zoos to bypass the obvious problems encountered when trying to arrange natural pregnancies between animals in different locations. Noted Benirschke, "It is extraordinarily expensive, difficult, and dangerous to ship, let's say, a male Indian rhino from San Diego to London in order to breed another animal. Yet, we know we must minimize the chances of inbreeding whenever possible. So, I look forward to the day when we can take semen out of the freezer and simply ship it to other zoos, and they will have the necessary reproductive knowledge of their animals to use this semen effectively. This is another reason why we monitor as many of our animals as possible who have had successful pregnancies or who we know are normal, so that we can gear up for this necessity of artificial insemination."

Zoo scientists in San Diego and elsewhere are already experimenting with embryo transfers, yet another method of propagation that bypasses traditional problem areas. "In 1980," Benirschke noted, "some 17,000 cattle in the country were conceived by fertilized egg transfer. If it's that easy in cattle, it ought to be possible in bongo and other exotic animals, given enough research activity." He envisions the day, perhaps around 1990, when frozen embryo exchanges will replace the transportation of animals on breeding loans between zoos. Equally amazing, an embryo would not have to be implanted into a female of the same species as itself. "When embryos become available," he said, "domestic animals will be able to serve as surrogate mothers for some of the exotic species. I would say that the physiologies are sufficiently similar for a zebra to grow in a horse, a buffalo in a cow, and so forth." One notable success came in 1981 at the Bronx Zoo, when a Holstein dairy cow gave birth to a gaur (a rare type of wild ox from Asia) following an embryo transfer.

In San Diego, reproductive physiologist Barbara Durrant has been pioneering techniques for embryo transfers between certain exotic animal species, particularly within the oryx family. Adapting methods first developed by the cattle industry, she hopes to implant Arabian oryx embryos into the wombs of less-endangered species.

Basically, the embryo transfer process starts when a female is superovulated with a hormone drug (Pregnant Mare's Serum Gonadotropin), which results in her releasing perhaps six or ten eggs instead of the normal one. After ovulation, she is mated and her embryos are given a chance to mature. About a week or two later, her oviducts are flushed out or the embryos are surgically removed and they are then either transferred immediately into the uterus of a waiting surrogate mother or mothers, or frozen for future use until an appropriate recipient can be found. "Superovulation increases a female's potential genetic contribution to her species," said Durrant, "and nonsurgical collection facilitates embryo recovery several times a year from any one female." Ideally, this is how many exotic animals will earn their keep in the future, acting either as donors or recipients.

This East African bongo and her calf represent one of the rarest animals on exhibit at the Zoo. Large, beautifully marked forest antelopes, few bongos are ever seen in the wild or in captivity. The Zoo obtained its first bongos in 1976 and five have been born since then.

Indian gaur are the largest of the wild cattle, and their only chance for survival will apparently be in parks and preserves. At the Bronx Zoo, a Holstein cow gave birth to a gaur in 1981 as a result of a successful artificial embryo transfer.

Benirschke regards the work by Durrant and researchers at other zoos as a prerequisite for saving the larger forms of creation. "It costs many thousands of dollars to buy and transport a single Indian rhino to this country for breeding. How much better it would be if we could divide those potential funds into two allotments: one to be used for a crash program in rhino husbandry, so we could know as much about their physiological requirements as we already know about domestic livestock, and the second to be used to expand on the embryological work already being done. Eventually, we would have the knowledge and techniques to implant embryos from any of the endangered Indian rhinos into the more common white rhino females. That would enable us to produce offspring for a fraction of the cost, and with a far greater certainty of success."

Perhaps the most far-reaching element in San Diego's research effort is Benirschke's internationally acclaimed "Frozen Zoo" cell bank for endangered species. This is a fascinating project that, at present, Benirschke would prefer to downplay for fear that the public will expect too much too soon and that, if disappointed, will be loath to contribute to future research efforts. "We lose face if we fail to attain our research goals in the time span advertised," he stressed. "Research is often talked about, but it's difficult for the layman to perceive just how slowly and cumulatively research proceeds, and how we can work for months and even years on a project until we get a sudden breakthrough that opens up a new way of working with a group of animals." Basically, Benirschke and his colleagues want to concentrate on building the baseline research that will one day enable the Frozen Zoo to contribute greatly to the survival of exotic animals—and hence to the survival of zoos themselves.

The Frozen Zoo, at present, consists of two stainless steel freezers which contain several dozen boxes of small plastic vials in which living cells, semen samples, and embryos are being stored for future use. The skin cells of over 350 different animals from 120 species are currently being maintained and can be thawed and used in genetic and hereditary studies conducted by members of the Zoo's Research Department. These tissue cultures (which are the result of skin biopsies performed or ear notches taken when an animal dies or has been anesthetized for veterinary treatment or shipment) also contain all of the hereditary information that might prove useful to future scientists when they are studying species whose survival is in jeopardy in their own time. This reflects Benirschke's belief that a major responsibility of the Zoo is to save as much genetic information as possible, in anticipation of the day when a particular animal that has become extinct in the wild will be reintroduced to the wild from a captive environment.

Also in storage is frozen semen from over twenty species, including the cheetah, Arabian oryx, orangutan, lowland gorilla, pygmy chimpanzee, purple-faced langur, Przewalski's horse, and okapi. "Once successfully frozen, there is no deterioration of sperm," Benirschke noted. "Bull semen, frozen twenty years ago, has recently been unfrozen and is still viable." Researchers foresee the day when they will be able to exchange sperm and eggs with other zoos, and create test-tube babies by drawing on these sperm and eggs, fertilizing them, and then cultivating the resulting embryo.

By utilizing urine collection and analysis of appropriate hormones, the Zoo's endocrinologists can project a female's precise time of ovulation; determine early on whether she is pregnant; then, if she is, monitor the progress of her pregnancy without causing stress to the animal. This allows for proper management throughout a female's pregnancy, from the early stages of appraising fetal well-being up to and including the time of delivery. The usefulness of these recent research efforts was illustrated by a case involving the douc langur, a beautiful, rare species of monkey from Vietnam. As veterinarian Phil Robinson noted, "A major problem has always been to detect if and when the fetus dies, particularly in more delicate species, since this can prove life-threatening to the expectant mother." The problem of miscarriages in the late stages of pregnancy had plagued douc langur reproduction in the past, so in 1978, when the group's adult female was found to be pregnant, her condition was monitored, utilizing urinary estrogen measurements. One day, suddenly, her hormone levels indicated that she was no longer pregnant. A caesarean section was performed and the dead fetus removed—very likely saving the mother's life.

Knowing that a birth is imminent, keepers will often isolate the mother-to-be and even post a twenty-four-hour watch for the more endangered species. They do this realizing that, otherwise, all the research efforts that went into the particular

Crowned cranes are monomorphic birds, meaning that the external appearance of the male and the female is identical.

Kookaburras, shown here on a branch "laughing," are also monomorphic birds.

never pulled the baby up to her chest so it could nurse." Subsequently, the keepers had to pull the infant for hand-raising at the Zoo nursery.

At the Wild Animal Park, veterinarians, keepers, and researchers gave even greater attention to the gorilla Dolly when she was pregnant with her fourth baby, Mary Ellen. Dolly's previous baby had been stillborn, so when daily monitorings of her urinary estrogens showed abnormally low levels in relation to her projected delivery date, officials feared that there might again be a problem. Amniocentesis and ultrasound tests were conducted, and both indicated that Dolly's baby was healthy—but not yet matured to the point that had been expected. Her delivery date was moved back several weeks and she was kept off exhibit so that keepers and vets could continue to monitor the pregnancy and, eventually, the postdelivery health of mother and baby.

Like many scientific advances, the ability to determine an exotic animal's reproductive stages—from ovulation through pregnancy—actually resulted from research directed toward another goal, that of trying to ascertain the sex of the nearly thirty percent of all bird species that are monomorphic, meaning birds in which both sexes have identical plumage, and which thus cannot be differentiated according to external appearance. This had proved a great hindrance to captive-breeding programs in two important ways. First, zoo keepers and

pregnancy could be futile, though, in a larger sense, not wasted. ("We learn something important from every disappointment," said Benirschke.) For example, in 1981, as part of the Zoo's orangutan breeding program, keepers maintained a twenty-four watch for eight days on Bubbles, who was about to have her third baby. A video camera was fixed on her cage, allowing her to give birth in privacy while keepers followed her progress and that of her baby by watching the television monitor that had been set up in their office below the orangutan bedrooms. This was particularly important because Bubbles's first two offspring had had to be hand-raised. "She didn't even want to hold her first kid," recalled keeper Gale Foland. "She took Jonathan and winged him across the cage, giving him a concussion, so we had to rush in and pull him out. This time she wasn't abusive, but it was good we had the watch because she did a poor job of cleaning off the amniotic sac and she

By studying a blood sample taken from this captured California condor chick, a monomorphic bird, researchers were able to determine that it was indeed a male. As a result of this early identification, the Park can now find an appropriate mate, thus hastening the chances of developing a viable captive population for this severely endangered species.

This gargoyle with the pineapple-shaped crown is actually a pair of palm cockatoos.

private aviculturists had to rely on blood samples or laparoscopy (a surgical procedure) to do the job, and both methods caused the birds stress that could result in injury or death. Second, in species which form pair bonds of long duration prior to successful mating, years of potential offspring could be lost by inadvertently placing two males or two females together.

So, when endocrinologist Bill Lasley and technician Nancy Czekala came to the Zoo in 1975, they were set to work on developing a nonstressful method of determining the sex of wild birds. They found that this could be done by analyzing a bird's droppings, which are a composite of urine and fecal wastes that contain both estrogen and testosterone, the female and male hormones. Sex determination could be fixed by looking at the ratio of these two steroids. This breakthrough tech-

nique was also effectively employed by researchers who needed to determine the estrous cycle of mammals, including primates.

The benefit of being able to distinguish the sex of monomorphic creatures was immediately appreciated by the Zoo's then curator of birds, K. C. Lint. With great fanfare, the Zoo had received a "breeding pair" of endangered, flightless kiwis in 1969. Looking like a large feather ball with two legs and a long bill, this is the national bird of New Zealand and is rarely seen in North American zoos, so San Diego was anxious to build a successful colony. The two birds were given a nice enclosure, but over the next eight years together they failed to produce a single egg. Then the Lasley-Czekala sexing system was applied, and the curator discovered he had two males. (The Zoo later coaxed two females out of New Zealand and

they laid eggs, but as none of these eggs hatched, it is now feared that the males are sterile, after all these years and efforts.)

When Lasley received the prestigious Rolex Award for Enterprise in Science for developing the bird-sexing technique, he donated the $26,000 in prize money to the Zoological Society of San Diego so that it could buy new equipment for an enlarged endocrinology laboratory. The expanded facilities, presently under the direction of Dr. Arden Bercovitz, have enabled the Zoo to provide a bird-sexing service for zoos and aviculturists around the world, with special attention being given to those zoos that have programs for rare or endangered species.

In order to tackle the problem of captive breeding from another research perspective, in 1980 Benirschke hired Dr. Donald Lindburg as the Zoo's first full-time animal behaviorist. A former college professor of anthropology, Lindburg is a world authority on the macaque, a family of omnivorous monkeys, which he studied in the wilds of India and Indonesia for three years. Not surprisingly, the Zoo's lion-tailed macaque colony, which has not fared well reproductively, has become one of his top priorities, for it is estimated that fewer than eight hundred lion-tails remain in the wild, and their future as a species depends upon the creation of numerous self-sustaining colonies in captivity. However, Lindburg also has important programs underway with cheetahs, tamarins, and slow lorises (a primate), hoping that behavioral insights can help nature take its course whenever possible.

Striving to improve overall breeding records throughout the Society's collection, Lindburg and the Research Department have chosen the lion-tailed macaque to test a strategy they believe will have broad applications for all zoos. "Essentially," said Lindburg, "we are focusing on each animal in our breeding program to try to determine its reproductive potential. Why invest perhaps years of effort and expense, while wasting your male's efforts, by keeping a female that's never going to reproduce—like the lion-tail in our own colony who was found to have no ovaries? Yet this happens all the time in zoos because people don't really know an animal's reproductive status. Thus, they end up with females in 'breeding' groups who live with a male for years but no reproduction occurs, even after they bring in a change of males."

Lion-tailed macaque and her baby

Davey, a white-lipped tamarin. Tamarins come from the jungles of South America and are only about the size of a small squirrel.

San Diego's strategy has been to give each lion-tailed macaque a complete physical examination, while also drawing blood or taking a skin biopsy for chromosomal study. In females, physiological testing (daily urine monitoring, for example) then reveals whether or not she is a functioning female, in terms of ovulation, ability to conceive, and so on. "If we determine that we have a fertile female, but no reproduction is taking place, then we know the problem is due to some social or behavioral impediment, such as an unwillingness to copulate," Lindburg explained. "We can then pursue one of several alternatives: bypass the behavioral deficit by using artificial insemination, try to discover the cause of the pathology, or attempt to modify the animal's behavior. Ultimately, we hope to take animals who are currently outside the existing gene pool or any breeding program and rehabilitate them, either physiologically or behaviorally, so they can become functioning, reproducing animals. I think that's a crucial breakthrough to make when you're working with an endangered species and you need every animal you can get."

Lindburg's initial research projects have concentrated on female fertility, but in the future he knows he must focus on male fertility as well. "When a captive population is reduced to just several hundred animals, you obviously aggravate the problem of genetic variability by failing to use certain males," he explained. "For example, we have a beautiful male lion-tail off exhibit, but he has been living by himself for ten years because he's hyperaggressive and we can't trust him with females. It's sad to have an animal like that who's not contributing reproductively, but our colony is not yet secure enough to risk losing a female. So we've collected his semen for artificial insemination—which hasn't worked yet—and we plan to spend a great deal of time trying to modify his behavior."

Yet another research project involves finding the correlation between a female's behavioral patterns and her estrous cycle. If this can be done, it will immeasurably aid human attempts at matchmaking among zoo animals. By observing and recording a female's daily behavior while also collecting urine samples to monitor her physiological state, it is hoped that the connection between the two will become obvious. Researcher Mary Meador is currently trying to establish the basic behavioral and endocrine parameters for white-lipped tamarins. "Ideally, she will be able to detect the peak of the female's cycle just on the basis of behavioral observation," said Lindburg, "and we'll be able to make this baseline information available to other breeders. Down the road, with the tamarins and many other animals, we should be able to say, 'For this particular species, we have identified the following behaviors or changes in behavior that normally reflect the fertile part of the cycle.' This kind of knowledge will be invaluable not only to our zoological society, but to all zoos, since many of them will not be able to afford to build endocrinology labs or to monitor their females."

Of course, just because reproductive behavior may correlate nicely with changes in physiological state for one female, this does not mean that the same will hold true for the rest of her species. Each animal will respond differently to increasing amounts of estrogen in the system. "This will never be totally reliable information from animal to animal," Lindburg admitted, "but even a little bit of help in this direction is important. One current example would be Samantha, the female gorilla, who slaps her rear end on the day that she ovulates. We've confirmed this through Dr. Lasley's urine studies. There's a slight variability, but she comes close enough, and if you wanted to mate her on the day that she ovulated, she would tell you by her behavior. Unfortunately, some female gorillas don't do anything at the peak of estrus, while others give off different indications."

As the availability and importation of wild-born exotic animals becomes increasingly rare and expensive, the specter of inbreeding haunts the Zoological Society of San Diego and zoos everywhere. "Basically," said Kurt Benirschke, "there are very few exotic animals coming in from the wild, and the situation can only worsen, so we're left with those that are now in zoos and wildlife reserves around the world." Benirschke's researchers are thus working with the curatorial staff not only to increase the number of captive animals within a species from one generation to the next, but also to safeguard genetic diversity as best as possible.

While some exotic species in captivity have proven resilient despite inbreeding (which tends to unmask recessive genes that can cause defects, some lethal), deleterious effects have been seen in such species as lemurs, who may be born with "funnel," or concave, chest, and Przewalski's horses, who may develop a crippling dysplasia of the hip. "There are exceptions," Jim Dolan noted. "The Himalayan tahr in the United

The Park's slender-horned gazelles are a true desert species, at home in sand-dune regions in which few other mammals can survive. They were once the most numerous of all Saharan mammals, but are now feared to be near extinction in the wild.

States probably haven't had any fresh blood in them since about 1910, yet they still breed very well and we haven't seen any inbreeding problems. But we're worried about their cousins, the Nilgiri tahr. All the animals in captivity in the U.S. today are descended from a group of just five animals that was shipped to the Memphis Zoo in 1972. There are none in captivity in Europe, and the only other captive group I know of is in India, which presents quarantine problems because of the animal diseases that occur over there. So it doesn't look good in terms of getting fresh, outcross [unrelated] animals.''

Like the Nilgiri tahr, the fifty-odd slender-horned gazelles in captivity trace back to a small genetic base, and the animals at the Wild Animal Park are beginning to show suspicious signs of inbreeding. "We're seeing a variety of physical problems that may be attributed to inbreeding—notably, a high mortality rate in the calves, and a high proportion of male offspring," said curator Carmi Penny. "Other captive species have started out with small founding populations like ours and have done quite well, so we apparently have an inbreeding problem combined with a sensitivity on the part of the species to competition within the exhibit."

All the slender-horned gazelles in the United States today descend from a founding population of five animals originally sent from a Tunisian zoo to Busch Gardens in Tampa, Florida. San Diego received a pair in 1968 and, with progeny from that pair and additional stock from Tampa, built a herd of nearly thirty animals at the Wild Animal Park by 1977. "Unfortunately," Dolan pointed out, "we were sitting with the entire captive world population—nobody else had any by then—and if we had lost them to illness or whatever, it's highly unlikely we could have replaced them. Even at that time they may have been extinct in the wild." So, three animals were sent to the New York Zoological Society's facility on St. Catherines Island, off the coast of Georgia, and other shipments have followed to the Dallas Zoo and the Living Desert Reserve in Palm Desert, California. "Now we can breathe a little easier," said Penny, who is international studbook keeper for the species (which means that he registers the pedigrees of all members of the species in captivity). "With the different groups now going, we can exchange animals and increase the variability within the gene pool."

When zoos start out with a small population of animals within a particular species, a certain degree of inbreeding is inevitably going to occur, but Dr. Oliver Ryder, the Zoo's geneticist, has been developing ways to decrease the level of inbreeding and thus minimize the potential problems. His work with the Przewalski's horse illustrates the cooperative strategy that will have to be adopted by all zoos if they intend to maintain a species in captivity for any length of time.

Ryder, coordinator of the North American Przewalski's Breeding Group, has become an expert at enlisting worldwide support for his fight to save this nearly extinct species, now found only in zoos and preserves. There are currently about 460 Przewalski's horses in captivity, all of whom have a complex, inbred family tree that dates back eleven generations. Yet, after Zoo researchers studied the genetics of all the horses in the Society's thriving collection (using blood samples and skin biopsies to analyze blood groups and chromosomes), Ryder wrote in ZOONOOZ: "Despite the fact that all Przewalski's horses in our collection trace their ancestry to nine individuals, our analyses indicate that considerable genetic variability has been retained."

Ryder uses a computer to help improve this diversity within the captive population, some of which is distributed in the dozen collections in the United States. He compiled a complete genealogy and now, using the computer to trace lineage, he can determine how closely two potential mates are related—and hence the advisability of such a mating. Having calculated the inbreeding coefficient (the measure of genetic variety or lack of it), he can give his blessing to this mating, or recommend another less-related mate, even though it might live several thousand miles away—or even across the Atlantic. Until artificial insemination is mastered, these "suggested" moves—expensive and time-consuming as they might be—will be necessary in order to safeguard the genetic makeup of future generations.

Even political diplomacy will be an important factor, since many of the remaining Przewalski's horses live in Czechoslovakia, the Soviet Union, and China. In May, 1981, three mares from the Wild Animal Park herd were flown to the Prague Zoo, halfway around the world, to rendezvous with a prized stallion named Bars in a mating maneuver that will ultimately foster genetic diversity both here and in Europe. "The stallion's mother, Orlitza III, was wild-caught in 1947 (and was, in fact, the last Przewalski's horse to be taken from the wild)," Ryder explained, "and her bloodline is unrepresented in North American collections. Since Bars is considered too valuable to be shipped here, we have to send the mares to him and bring them back pregnant. The risks are minimal [pregnant domestic horses are regularly shipped great distances] and they are necessary for the sake of the species." Under the terms of this exchange, Prague will keep the first three foals and then send the mares back to San Diego once they are pregnant again. Another around-the-world horse trade took place in 1982 when the United States and the Soviet Union, after years of negotiation, swapped six horses. San

About fifteen Przewalski's horses are maintained at the Park, in two separate breeding groups. Somewhat shorter than domestic horses, the Przewalski's horse is a stocky animal with an erect mane, long tail, and no forelock.

Diego, in conjunction with the Bronx Zoo, sent three horses and the Russians sent a shipment that included a prized stallion, Vulkan, whose mother was also Orlitza III. The introduction of Bars's and Vulkan's bloodline into the United States group of less than a hundred horses will lower the current inbreeding coefficient to a more acceptable level.

Yet another way Zoo researchers are cooperating with the Society's curators to help ensure a future for endangered species is through their work with off-exhibit breeding groups. Such groups enable the Society to maintain a larger overall population of selected species—thus broadening the gene pool of captive species—and also provide offspring that can be sent to other zoos or used to replace animals in the main exhibits.

At present, the Research Department's most visible role is with the primates assigned to the off-exhibit Primate Pad, a

This is one of five pads comprising the Primate Propagation Center, located on a hillside behind the Zoo hospital. These off-exhibit enclosures will help the Zoo become more self-sufficient in terms of breeding the smaller primate species.

series of enclosures located behind the Zoo hospital and adjacent to the Primate Propagation Center. Here, researchers are assessing the genetic and physiological characteristics of various animals. "Eventually," said Benirschke, "we hope to be sophisticated enough in our methods that we can select the most promising brood stock for off-exhibit breeding groups while assigning weaker genetic stock to the public exhibits [along with surplus or postreproductive animals]. If we get reproduction from the animals on exhibit, that's great, but

Red ruffed lemur

A ring-tailed lemur baby rides piggyback on its mother.

basically they will help pay the bills while the off-exhibit animals—we hope—get the job done biologically."

Lemurs are not a household name in zoos around the world, but their plight in the wild and the efforts to ensure a future for them in captivity symbolize many of the issues involved today as researchers try to save valuable species from extinction.

A beautiful and gentle primate with large eyes and distinctive foxlike muzzles, most lemurs have thick fur coats and long, bushy tails. Almost all of the twenty surviving species in the wild are tree dwellers and all of them live solely on the island of Madagascar, off the southeast coast of Africa. Therein lies the problem, for even though Madagascar is a relatively large island—slightly smaller than the combined areas of California, Nevada, and Oregon—only *one-fifteenth* of its once vast

rain forest remains standing today, thanks to deforestation by the natives and by large-scale commercial enterprises from foreign countries. The remaining forests are fast disappearing, eating away at the lemur's habitat, while hunting goes virtually unchecked despite the laws that exist to prevent it. While it is true that there are fourteen natural preserves, they are insufficiently patrolled, they have human populations living within their boundaries, they are scattered throughout the island, and they are too small to serve as a permanent refuge for those lemurs which somehow manage to survive through the 1980s. In fact, so much of Madagascar lies in ruin today, and the population trends are so inexorable, that zoologists sadly concede that the lemur family will come to an abrupt and final end there—in the wild, that is—by the early 1990s. Compounding the problem is the fact that, at present, the Madagascan government is not allowing the exportation of

Black-and-white ruffed lemur

lemurs. "Madagascar is gone," said Benirschke, "and unique animals like the lemur will not survive there. The only chance that lemurs have for at least relative survival is through efforts made here and at other zoos."

The concern for lemurs and their ultimate survival goes way beyond the practical and aesthetic considerations normally associated with the regret felt when a species in the wild becomes extinct. For one thing, lemurs are an extraordinary source of information concerning evolution. They are prosimians, animals which preceded in evolution the true primates, who in turn culminated in man. Lemur fossils dating back fifty million years have been found in North and South America, Asia, Europe, and Africa. Competition with higher forms of primates and predators eventually did away with these early lemur forms everywhere except on the island of Madagascar, which was separated from the mainland of Africa as a result of a cataclysmic geologic rift. Here, isolated and with few predators or competitors, lemurs thrived and evolved into an astounding variety of species, undisturbed on "the island that time forgot" until man arrived. Centuries later, in 1967, field researcher Alison Jolly would ruefully note, "Madagascar's history is uniquely rich, a record of the dawn of the age of mammals, but it is difficult to hope that the lemurs, so full of clues to our own past, have themselves much future." A second reason to bemoan their loss is that lemurs have proven invaluable to medical research. Their extinction would deprive mankind of one of the few appropriate animal models that exist for studying liver cancer, hemachromatosis, and funnel chest—ailments that also afflict human beings.

Those lemur species which may eventually escape extinction (only eight of the twenty existing species are even found in zoos today, and of these eight, San Diego has four) will certainly benefit from the basic knowledge of them that is currently being gained through multidisciplinary studies at the San Diego Zoo.

Starting in the mid-1960s, the Zoo received several shipments (eight pairs in total) of red ruffed and black-and-white ruffed lemurs from Madagascar. "From those original animals we have bred close to 150 ruffed lemurs," said Diane Brockman, "which is a nice record. Unfortunately, by starting with a small original population, we're now seeing what, I feel, are the effects of inbreeding: funnel chest in offspring, babies that are underweight, and declining reproduction. Also, although

Black lemur

it's normal for lemurs to have twins and triplets, we've had a couple of quadruplet births here and in other zoos. Whether or not we can attribute these things to inbreeding, we know we must initiate exchanges with other zoos."

Brockman is also counting on research efforts at the Primate Pad to boost breeding success. "Lemurs breed fairly well, and the females conceive at three years, half the age of most primates," noted Benirschke, "but there are also problems we don't understand yet—like why some animals breed and others do not, and why there are incompatible pairs." So, the first studies ever of lemur reproductive cycles, genetics, and nutrition are now being conducted while behavioral work continues to proceed. Each lemur colony is being studied to ascertain the basic reproductive parameters of normal animals with the hope that this information can then be applied to help non-breeding animals. Artificial insemination is yet another alternative as the Zoological Society of San Diego tries to map a genetically sound strategy with which to perpetuate lemur species in captivity, even hundreds of years after the last one has died in Madagascar.

Should conditions on that island change in the ensuing centuries, allowing the regeneration of a substantial, protected tropical forest habitat, the descendants of lemurs in captivity today could be called upon to repopulate that patch of wilderness. In the meantime, generations and generations of animal lovers will still be able to share the wide-eyed wonder of the lemur.

Wherever animals live in the wild today, their continued existence is imperiled by man's devastating encroachments. Ensuring the survival of as many species as possible is a global challenge for conservationists, governments, and native populations alike, but zoological societies everywhere are also play-ing a vital role. "We cannot hope to save every endangered species," said Tom Foose, conservation coordinator for the American Association of Zoological Parks and Aquariums. "But for those species we can save, zoos must be an ark, a place where animals can survive even when their natural habitat has disappeared."

Beyond this, a zoo's protected environment allows for detailed, ongoing research projects and breeding programs that are not possible in the wild. "Many types of research can *only* be accomplished in captive populations," noted Kurt Benirschke. "Access to the blood and chromosomes of wild species is virtually impossible in free-ranging wild populations. But most animals, sooner or later, come through the doors of zoos where meaningful study can be accomplished and we have the freedom to take action in these animals' behalf."

With a comprehensive, innovative research program already underway, the San Diego Zoo is at the forefront of efforts by zoos to narrow the gap between current abilities and optimistic aspirations regarding reproduction among captive animals. Utilizing continued breakthroughs in the science of animal husbandry and aided by the Society's large and varied animal collection, the Zoo has become a wildlife research center, providing leadership, scientific support, and an international perspective as it cooperates with other zoos to help buffer hundreds of species against the forces of extinction.

Meanwhile, though 800 acres have been developed at the Wild Animal Park, another 1,000 acres can still be utilized to accommodate continued growth by species already within the Society's collection and to provide a sanctuary for additional new species. Working together, the Zoo and the Wild Animal Park will continue to provide creative and humane animal management, preserving a priceless animal collection that will enrich the lives of generations to come.

According to current estimates, Sumatran tigers will be extinct in the wild by the year 2000. Only 500 now survive in their native range and less than 150 exist in captivity. Thus, one of the most important propagation efforts at the Park involves a small group of Sumatran tigers who were imported from East Germany in 1979. The tigers reside in a heavily planted, three-acre enclosure in view of the passing monorail. This jungle-like exhibit allows for seclusion and provides ample room for anticipated offspring to grow and thrive.

These two South African cheetahs at the Park are part of an
extensive research program designed to learn more about the
species' social and reproductive
physiology.

Three cheetah litters yielded eight cubs in 1982. This particular mother, Cleo, raised her cubs in an enclosure that was visible to the public from the Kilimanjaro Hiking Trail at the Park. Other cheetahs are maintained in a fifteen-acre off-exhibit area near the hospital.

THE NEXT GENERATION

Top, left to right:
Gaboon vipers
Jackson's chameleons
American flamingos
Black-necked swans
African elephants

Right:
Helmeted guineafowl

INDEX

All numbers in this index refer to page numbers; those in italic type indicate illustrations.

ACKNOWLEDGMENTS

Working on this book was an unusually rewarding experience, personally and professionally, and I would like to give special thanks to those who helped make it so:

Charles Bieler, executive director of the Zoological Society of San Diego, who encouraged me to report and write the story I wanted to tell.

The curators at the San Diego Zoo and the San Diego Wild Animal Park—James Dolan, Ph.D.; Carmi Penny; Larry Killmar; Diane Brockman; Arthur C. Risser, Jr., Ph.D.; Kerry Muller; and James P. Bacon, Jr., Ph.D.—who talked thoughtfully and candidly about their jobs and the treasured animals in their care.

The many keepers, veterinarians, and researchers who provided behind-the-scenes insights and who conveyed such a deep commitment to wildlife conservation: especially Jane Jacobson; Sue Kennedy; Earl T. Schultz; Rick Barongi; Randy Rieches; Philip T. Robinson, D.V.M.; Jane Meier, D.V.M.; Lester Nelson, D.V.M.; Kurt Benirschke, M.D.; and Donald Lindburg, Ph.D.

Carole Towne, who played a pivotal role from the very beginning of this project, and whose expert public-relations staff was helpful in many important ways.

Marjorie Shaw, editor of the justly respected ZOONOOZ, who contributed valuable editorial perspective.

Susan Hathaway, Terry Ashford, and F. D. Schmidt, who were industrious and persevering through months of photo selection.

Ron Garrison, to whose talent this book is a tribute.

John Boswell, my agent, who gave me the chance to write about a subject that proved to be endlessly intriguing and challenging.

My publisher, who never compromised quality to expediency, and especially Margaret Kaplan, who initiated the idea for this book and who coordinated the effort that followed with thoughtful direction; Sheila Franklin, my editor, who displayed an enviable ability to shepherd a manuscript and photographs from one stage to the next with unfailing good cheer, encouragement, persistence, and sound judgment; and designer Bob McKee, who integrated the text and photographs with skill and imagination.

My wife, Pam, whose continual interest in this book strengthened my motivation, and our children, Alan and Allison—and children everywhere—in hopes that wildlife will always remain a vital part of their world.

Bill Bruns

Unless otherwise specified, all photographs were taken by Ron Garrison, photographic services supervisor at the San Diego Zoo. Photographs from other sources (listed by page number) are gratefully acknowledged below.

Terry Ashford: 203; Diane Brockman: 150–51; Allan Hancock Foundation: 38, 39; Dan Hoyer: 82 below; Bill Noonan: 46 all; F. D. Schmidt: 4, 5, 9, 49, 55, 56, 71, 74, 94, 104, 116, 117 both, 166, 174 both, 175, 176, 187, 211, 234 above, 235 both, 236, 275; Union-Tribune Publishing Co.: 34; R. Van Nostrand: 10, 162–63, 260, 272; Archives of the Zoological Society of San Diego: 30, 32, 35, 36, 41, 42, 53, 54 both, 61, 62, 86, 87, 88, 208 all, 209.